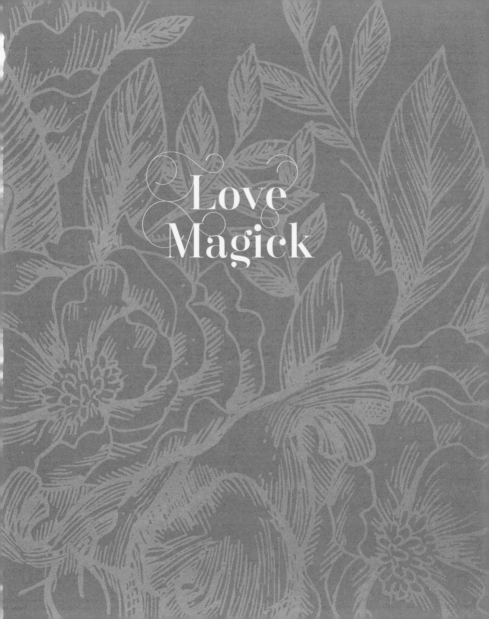

Love
Magick

Love Magick

Spells for Amour

CASSANDRA EASON

AUTHOR OF *1001 SPELLS*

STERLING ETHOS
New York

STERLING ETHOS
New York

An Imprint of Sterling Publishing Co., Inc.
1166 Avenue of the Americas
New York, NY 10036

ISBN 978-1-4549-3348-9

Distributed in Canada by Sterling Publishing Co., Inc.
^{c}/o Canadian Manda Group, 664 Annette Street
Toronto, Ontario M6S 2C8, Canada
Distributed in the United Kingdom by GMC Distribution Services
Castle Place, 166 High Street, Lewes, East Sussex BN7 1XU, England
Distributed in Australia by NewSouth Books
University of New South Wales, Sydney, NSW 2052, Australia

For information about custom editions,
special sales, and premium and corporate purchases,
please contact Sterling Special Sales at 800-805-5489
or specialsales@sterlingpublishing.com.

Manufactured in China

2 4 6 8 10 9 7 5 3 1

sterlingpublishing.com

Cover design by Elizabeth Mihaltse Lindy
Interior design by Christine Heun, with Sharon Jacobs

Image Credits: iStock (throughout): PeterHermesFurian; imaginasty; olgagriga;
vectortatu; lllerlok_Xolms; SharonJacobs (throughout); Shutterstock: (cover, throughout)
Angie Makes; ararat.art; MysticalLink; Hein Nouwens; Pinchuk Oleksandra

Images on cover and throughout interior from Getty/iStock
Sigil art (cover) created using Sigilscribe (sigilscribe.me) by Metatronix

To my beloved family, Jade, Miranda, Tom, Jack,
Bill, Freya, Holly and Oliver, with special thanks to
Kate Zimmermann, Konnie, and John Gold,
who have all inspired and guided me.

Contents

Introduction

Love spells have existed throughout the millennia and in different cultures from ancient Sumeria and Egypt onward, for most people want someone special to love and to love them in return. Though some do meet their true love when young and remain together all their lives (many believe this person is our twin soul, our alter ego, whom we have met in other lifetimes), others find this twin soul love, with whom there may be instant recognition, later in life. It may even be a childhood sweetheart from whom we parted and meet years later after other unsuccessful relationships, to find the spark is still there. Indeed, social media has led to a rapid increase in these reconnections, and love online is an ever-growing means of finding the right partner for those whose immediate environment may be socially limited.

Love spells work in two ways, first by drawing us telepathically to the person who is right for us. If we have experienced unhappiness in love, we consciously or unconsciously close down our love energies and so don't attract love. Love spells open those energies to the right person. When you have been in a series of bad relationships because you are too loving and giving and attract flawed partners, I have suggested spells to open yourself to the right kind of love, rather than returning to someone who promises to change but never does.

But love magick also acts as an automatic radar, drawing us to the right place at the time when that right person will be waiting, often unexpectedly.

Many who are drawn to a particular place where they meet their true love didn't expect to be there at all; synchronicity or meaningful coincidence drew them together, strengthened by a love spell.

Love magick too can clear away a redundant or destructive love or the lingering hopes that, in spite of numerous betrayals, our partner will change for the better. Also in the book are spells to increase commitment in love and make a relationship permanent, if a potential partner has been hurt or is tied by other commitments to a past or dying unhappy relationship that needs resolving.

But reconciliation to start again after a betrayal or interference by others, where there is still love and goodwill, can be given a boost by spells to reopen the old channels but in a more positive way, especially where one partner is being stubborn, though s/he wants to try again.

Different chapters focus on love at various stages of life: teenage love; the frantic middle years, when in the modern world, not only may adult children remain in the nest but the older generation may need support. This can put stress on any loving relationship, especially when a couple was hoping to spread their wings. There is also a chapter on love in the golden years, where a new partner, perhaps after divorce or bereavement, may meet resistance from the previous partner's family or a partner wants to stay home while we long to sell up and explore the world. Passion and sex magick offer ways of rekindling physical and spiritual love when work, money worries, family, and routine have dampened the early ecstasy.

By rekindling connection with the cycles of the moon, a couple may relax and conceive, whether spontaneously or with medical help. Reliance on ovulation charts and making love according to the calendar, and not desire, may take away the magick of a relationship and, ironically, make conception harder. Fertility spells focus on rekindling that joy and passion.

WHAT YOU NEED FOR LOVE SPELLS

Each spell in the book contains a list of what you will need for spell-casting, most of which you already have in your cupboard or toolbox, or which can easily be obtained from the local supermarket, garden center, or home improvement store. There is no need to buy specialty magical equipment, as many spell items are in everyday use. Candle snuffers, for example, are generally found in stores that sell candles, but you can easily use metal tongs to snuff out a candle or the back of an old spoon, and so extinguish a love you wish to banish from your life.

As with all spells, I specify the ideal candle colors, crystals, and fragrances, but you can substitute for whatever you cannot obtain. Pearls and rose quartz are good for gentler love, green jade is the universal faithful love crystal, any red crystal is ideal for passion, orange carnelian works for fertility, and apache tears or smoky quartz—dark crystals through which light can be seen if they are held up to a source of illumination—relieve old sorrows.

So, too, will any floral fragrance substitute for specific ones in love magick, though rose, lavender, and chamomile—ideal love fragrances—are easily obtainable. Fragrant flowers or flower oil, such as the sensuous ylang-ylang, are powerful for calling love and passion.

You can use fresh petals plucked from a flower or potpourri in floral love spells. Herbal tea bags, split open, will offer a whole range of herbs and flowers often used in love magick, as will the cooking section of your local supermarket. Empower herbs in a love spell and afterwards use them in cooking a meal for your lover.

You may wish to keep on hand a box with different-colored candles, incense sticks, incense holders, lengths of thin curtain cord and ribbons for love knot spells, scissors, and a letter opener for carving symbols in the wax of unlit candles.

Green and pink candles call and keep love, red is for passion and driving off rivals, blue for fidelity, and silver for moon love magick. But you can substitute an all-purpose white.

Candles used to restore, attract, or increase love can be burned around the home in the days after the spell, though those used for banishing or binding should be disposed of after the spell in environmentally safe ways.

Look in advance for places where you can bury small items after a spell. Also, find a source of nearby running water to cast petals or seeds (if necessary, use a bucket or bowl of water and pour out the water on the ground) and a place where you can scatter seeds or petals into the air (even from an upstairs window). For fire, think barbecue coals, bonfires, or candles in deep holders, so you can safely burn threads and scatter salt or herbs in the flame. For major burning of paper, set the paper in a large heatproof bucket outdoors, half-filled with sand or soil, so you can safely burn the paper in the flame.

Pick up a current datebook, listing dates with daily moon phases and the zodiac signs through which the moon passes each month, or get access to a good online site, for example, https://www.moongiant.com/fullmoons, which gives you the universal moon times so you can work out the moon phases in your own location, or http://starsignstyle.com/full-moon-calendar, which contains the zodiac signs of the different full moons.

The moon is a very powerful energy source, in all its phases in love magick, as well as other kinds of magick.

HOW TO CAST SPELLS

You will need a space, a table, or any flat surface, indoors or out, on which to place all your ingredients before starting a spell. However, there is no need to keep this just for magick. If you want to create an altar, you can find full instructions on how to do this in *A Little Bit of Wicca* (Sterling Ethos). In practice, however, for informal spells the kitchen table has been the site and source where magick has been carried out by ordinary people and community wise women and men for daily needs for centuries.

Look in the appropriate section of the book for the right spell, using the index to narrow down your choices.

PROTECTION WHILE SPELL CASTING

While in formal or ritual magick, quite elaborate preparations may be called for, such as casting a circle and closing ceremonies, the spells in this book are informal and cast for a specific purpose, rather than as part of a magical celebration or offerings ceremony. The exception are the two versions of the ancient Holy Grail Ritual in chapter 11 that offers a beautiful and spiritual prelude to sex magick. If you want to know how to set up a spell more formally, my book, A Little Bit of Wicca, takes you through the process step by step.

But the spells in this and, indeed, my other Sterling Ethos spell books follow the tradition of folk magick, carried out with good intention to harm no one and therefore contain built-in protection.

However, if you wish, before beginning you can hold a pointed crystal quartz or a clear quartz crystal massage wand in your dominant hand and face the area where you will be casting your spell. Alternatively, you could use the index finger of your dominant hand with the second finger joined to it, pointed horizontally outward, or the whole hand, fingers together and pointing outward, and facing the area where you will be casting your spell.

Hold the crystal or hand outward straight ahead and visualize drawing around you, clockwise and including the spell area, a circle of shimmering light from the ground, rising up like walls of light extending above the whole space like a shimmering star (include yourself within the light), then fading but present throughout the spell. Ask silently, May only goodness and light enter here.

When you finish the spell, reverse the process and, if you used a pointed crystal, wash it under running water.

Alternatively, picture directly ahead of you, as you face the spell table or the outdoor space in which you will be working, Uriel, archangel of the earth, in indigo robes with his torch of fire; then, to your right-hand side, Raphael, the healer archangel, in his robes of early morning sunlight; behind you the glorious red and gold Michael, archangel of the sun; and to your left the starry Gabriel, archangel of the moon. Ask the four archangels to cast their shimmering light all around you and the spell area and picture this brilliance extending as a star of light over your head and including the spell table or outdoor space. Afterwards, thank the archangels and the light will fade to be reactivated whenever you call upon them.

USING THE RIGHT WORDS AND FORMAT

Read the spell two or three times before beginning, and feel free to change words or actions that don't feel right to you. Write down any key words you will be using and, if you wish, you can read the words during the spell. Memorize the order of the spell and have a run-through of the spell actions and words before starting to check that you have everything you need within reach. If possible, make sure you will be undisturbed unless someone is sharing the spell with you. Switch off all electronic devices or put them on silent and, unless it is a spell involving technological equipment, try to have these out of the room or cover them. All the spells can be cast equally effectively by male-female or same-sex partners, changing a word here or there to reflect your needs, if necessary.

For those who may be sharing a crowded apartment or facing the constant demands of small children, you can cast any of the spells in this book simply by reading them slowly at the appropriate time and visualizing them. For each spell is empowered in its creation and can be activated by the simple act of reading. Perhaps light a candle or hold an object you are going to endow as a protective charm as you read. It is possible with practice to do a spell entirely in your mind while working at home, taking a child to kindergarten, or in a noisy office. If you can memorize the words and say them in your mind, so much the better.

In the first chapter I have focused on spells to find your twin soul.

CHAPTER 1

Spells to Attract Your Twin Soul, a Soul Mate, and to Remove Soul Adversaries from Past and Present Worlds

Your twin soul or flame, whom you don't encounter in every lifetime, represents a love you may have experienced in other lifetimes and with whom you feel an instant deep connection, even though, in some cases, you may meet and part and meet again or even not connect until later in life. Twin soul relationships may be fraught with difficulty because in a particular lifetime, your twin soul may have a lesson to learn and so not be as spiritually ready to connect. Or s/he may have become entangled in a relationship with another person when you do meet, or you may live far away from one another. However, even if you don't settle with your twin soul this time around, it may be that you will find great happiness with a soul mate, a close member of the group of souls who travel with us throughout different incarnations. You may also meet soul adversaries, those who masquerade as twin souls, but after a period of initial happiness can begin to destroy your self-confidence and cause deep hurt.

Spells can help you to protect your sensitive soul and to meet the right mate, one who offers you respect and devotion, whether a twin soul relationship or a less intense but equally lovely soul mate, and protect you from the users and losers who may be attracted to, and ready to take advantage of, your generosity and kindness.

To Call Your Twin Soul Into Your Life

YOU WILL NEED

Two identical rose quartz hearts or crystals ★ A bowl of salt
★ A pink drawstring bag ★ Dried rose petals

TIMING

During the crescent moon

THE SPELL

* Outdoors, hold the crystals in your open, cupped hands, breathe on them, then say, *Twin soul, I know not where you may be, but your life I wish joined to me. Find me and let love daily grow, for when we meet I shall you know.*

* Bury the two hearts with salt in the drawstring bag, marking the spot with scattered rose petals, saying, *Our love shall grow deep, Mother Earth. As we sleep, give our love birth.*

* After 48 hours dig up the crystals, wash and dry them, putting them in the bag with the remaining rose petals.

* Keep the bag near your bed.

If You Meet Your Twin Soul But S/He
Is Already in a Relationship

YOU WILL NEED

Modeling clay, adding a drop of rose oil to the
clay ∗ Pink ribbon ∗ A pink silk scarf

TIMING

The end of the moon cycle

THE SPELL

∗ Create two figures with the clay.

∗ With the ribbon, tie the figures face-to-face with three loose knots,
saying, *Twin Soul, I call you to my side, when it is right to be. That you
will see, I am your love, and come willingly to me.*

∗ Untie the knots, holding one figure in each hand, and say, *The bonds
of love I do untie. Only you can make the choice. But when you are ready,
I will be waiting, and you will hear my voice.*

∗ Wrap the clay figures together in the scarf, securing the scarf with
the ribbon in a loose bow.

∗ Keep them until the clay crumbles.

To Rekindle Love From a Previous Lifetime if You Feel Instant Recognition with Someone New

YOU WILL NEED

A space between two trees where you can sit quietly ∗ Two pink and green unakite crystals, the twin soul stones ∗ A necklace finding

TIMING

If possible, on a misty day or in soft sunlight

THE SPELL

∗ Sit between the trees, holding the crystals in your closed hands and say, *Between the worlds I call you, through the mists of time. Recall, reconnect, return in love. Remember how once you were mine.*

∗ Bury one of the unakite crystals in the center of the space, saying, *I call back our love through this gateway of time. When you see the twin crystal, you'll recall you are mine.*

∗ Attach the second unakite to a necklace finding and wear it as a pendant whenever you meet next.

If You Fear That You Have Lost Your Twin Soul in This Life and Suspect This May Also Have Happened in an Earlier Lifetime

TIMING

After a bad quarrel or if your love has backed off

THE SPELL

* Unravel the yarn and tie one end to the back of a chair, saying,
  The link between us once unraveled. Since then through many lives we've traveled. I will not lose you ever again. This love once reconnected, lasting shall remain.

* Wind the yarn around your hands, saying softly and continuously,
  I reconnect with you, [Name,] *unbreakably. That in this lifetime together can we be, happily and permanently.*

* Untie the knot from the chair and secure the skein with green ribbon, keeping it in a safe place where it cannot be unraveled.

* Reestablish friendly contact.

If You Have a Chance Later in Life to Reconnect With an Earlier Twin Soul Love or Childhood Sweetheart

YOU WILL NEED

A photo of the two of you together when young and also a recent photo ✶ Seven green candles in a triangle, two at the bottom, two on either side and one at the apex, with the photos in the center.

TIMING

If you are hesitating

THE SPELL

✶ Light each of the candles, zigzagging bottom to top, left to right, saying, *Can the lightning flash of love strike twice? Can the Flame once dim, grow strong? Why should we hesitate? I have loved you my whole life long.*

✶ Extinguish the candles, placing the second photo face down on top of the first.

✶ Relight the candles, saying, *Twice as precious, a second chance, rekindled twin love, much more than romance.*

✶ Leave the candles burning.

✶ Afterward frame the photos side by side.

If You Are Always Breaking Precious Items or Equipment at Home or Work

YOU WILL NEED

A delicate precious item from within the home
★ A large feather

TIMING

Saturday, the day of caution

THE SPELL

* Stand in front of, but not too near the precious item.

* Gently waft the feather in front of it, but not too close, saying softly and rhythmically, *Cautiously, gently, softly, do not shatter, do not break. Do not splinter or cease to work under my touch, I ask this much.*

* Continue to walk around the home with the feather in front of anything valuable and fragile, repeating the spell words and actions.

* If office equipment ceases to function the minute you touch it, before using it gently and surreptitiously move your dominant hand vertically nine times in front of it and say the spell words nine times in your mind, then approach it slowly and calmly.

A Charm Bag to Keep
Misfortune From Your Life

YOU WILL NEED

Five of the following: allspice, basil, chamomile, dill, juniper berries,
lavender, lemon balm (Melissa), rosemary, thyme, or vetivert
✴ A bowl and a spoon ✴ A green drawstring bag or purse
✴ Five golden-colored coins or green currency notes ✴ Salt
✴ Five hairs from your head ✴ Patchouli or sandalwood oil

TIMING

The day before the crescent moon

THE SPELL

✴ Add the herbs one by one into the bowl, mixing with the spoon after
each addition, first counterclockwise, then clockwise, five times each
way, saying, *Five by five, the spell's alive. Bad fortune shall no longer be.
Only good luck may come to me.*

✴ Place the herbs in the bag. Add the coins, five pinches of salt, and the
hairs, blending with a few drops of oil and saying, *Five by five, in
vain bad fortune strive. This bag shall be, guardian of good luck, health,
and prosperity.*

✴ Close the bag, hiding it where it will not be discovered. Replace the
contents when the bag loses its fragrance and use the bag until good
luck shines on the person casting the spell.

To Change Bad Luck into Good, Using the Waning and Crescent Moon

YOU WILL NEED

A glass bowl of water ★ White or apple cider vinegar ★ Dried rosemary thyme, sage, and mint

TIMING

After dark, at the end of the waning moon cycle

THE SPELL

* Take the bowl outdoors and to the water add nine drops of vinegar and a handful of herbs.

* Swirl the bowl in both directions alternately, saying, *Bad luck, I give you to Grandmother Moon, to take away all sorrow and bring better tomorrows, very soon.*

* Dip your index finger in the water and lick it, saying, *Grandmother, I take in your power, to transform misfortune at this hour.*

* Leave the bowl in a sheltered place, and once you see the crescent moon in the sky, pour the water onto the ground, saying, *All misfortune I pour away, rising moon, bring good luck to stay.*

To Break a Specific Run
of Bad Luck in Your Life

YOU WILL NEED

Make a calendar with a numbered square for each day of
the current year up to the present day marked in pencil,
starting with the time the ill luck began * An eraser
* A sharp scissors * A new store-bought calendar

TIMING

The end of a week

THE SPELL

* Go from the present day backwards and erase each square number, saying, *Misfortune I erase, unlucky nights and days. Unwritten as though they never had been, no longer in my life shall bad luck be seen.*

* When the squares are empty, cut up the squares from the present day to the beginning of the year, saying, *Cut up, banished, disappeared, ahead lie fortunate days, months, and lucky years.*

* Burn the cut-up squares and hang the new calendar on the wall, marking the present day as THE BEST DAY EVER.

To Avert Bad Luck If You Have Broken a Lucky Talisman or a Mirror, Which Traditionally Brings Seven Years of Bad Luck

YOU WILL NEED

The broken pieces ✶ A strong dark piece of cloth ✶ Dried tarragon, the protective dragon's herb ✶ A piece of dark-colored string ✶ A soft white cloth

TIMING

After the breakage

THE SPELL

* Set the broken pieces on the dark cloth and sprinkle tarragon on top, saying, *Seven years of bad luck are not to be, misfortune come not after me.*

* Wrap the broken pieces securely in the dark-colored cloth and tie it with four knots of the dark-colored string, one on top of the other, saying, *Four square, locked and bound around, no trace in my life of bad luck s hall be found.*

* Put the parcel on a high, dark shelf for seven years.

* Buy a new mirror or an identical talisman, and polish it with a soft white cloth, saying, *Light enter this mirror/charm and shine. Henceforward, good fortune shall be mine.*

To Start Again If You Have Been Unlucky for Most of Your Life

Peppercorns ✳ Rosemary ✳ Sage ✳ Dried cloves ✳ A small
jug of apple cider vinegar ✳ A larger jug of water in which
rose petals have been soaked for a few hours

TIMING

The end of a day, week, or month

THE SPELL

✳ Add the peppercorns, rosemary, sage, and cloves to the jug with the
vinegar and swirl the jug three times each way, saying, *Bad luck too long
has lingered in my life, obstructing my path and causing me strife.*

✳ Go out of your front door and pour the vinegar in a thin line, right to
left, ahead of you as you stand close to and facing away from the door.

✳ Now, standing even closer to the front door, ahead of you, left to right,
pour the rose water in a line, saying, *New life, new fortune begins from
here. Good luck is mine, I have drawn the line.*

13

If You Lose a Lucky Charm and
Fear the End of Good Fortune

A replacement of the lost charm, as closely resembling the lost item
as possible ⋆ A small sealable cloth bag ⋆ A sealable bag of salt

TIMING

The new moon before it becomes visible in the sky

THE SPELL

* Hold the replacement item between your open-cupped hands, close
  your hands over it and say, *I impress you, no less, with accumulated
  good fortune, I have gained in the past, and this time will last. Good luck
  passes through me to you, as the new moon grows it shall be so, and
  good luck regrow.*

* Wrap the charm in the cloth bag, enclose that bag in the bag of salt, and
  bury it, marking the place. Dig it up when the crescent moon can be
  seen in the sky.

* Throw away the bag of salt and carry your new charm with confidence.

To Avert Bad Luck If Your Personal Astrological Chart Is Against You or Mercury Is in Retrograde

Note: People would already know the stars were unlucky or they would not be doing this spell in the first place.

YOU WILL NEED

A long strip of paper on which is written in red ink,
I SHALL BE LUCKY WHATEVER THE STARS SAY. (You can check your stars or Mercury position online or in the astrological section of any daily journal.) ⋆ A clear glass jar or a bottle with a lid ⋆ A pile of precut short red threads ⋆ A chopped clove of garlic

TIMING

Just before the unfavorable positions occur

THE SPELL

* Push the paper right down into the jar, saying, *These unfortunate stars in my life I repel. This day/period my fortunes shall go well. Banished be, effects that might be bad for me.*

* Add the threads and then the chopped garlic so the jar is packed.

* Seal it and bury it in a marked place until the star positions become favorable.

* Dig it up and dispose of the jar and its contents intact.

A Friday the Thirteenth Protection Ritual

A lucky charm or a favorite piece of jewelry ✳ A bowl of salt

TIMING

Late in the evening of the twelfth

THE SPELL

✳ Find a flat surface where your charm won't be disturbed until the fourteenth.

✳ Make thirteen circles of salt, moving outward, each counterclockwise around the charm, saying, *Thirteen, lucky thirteen, tomorrow shall be seen. Outstanding opportunity, as good luck flows to me.*

✳ Touch the charm within the circles and say, *Hold misfortune on the morrow, bring joy, harmony, and no sorrow. Friday the thirteenth will go for me, absolutely splendidly.*

✳ On the fourteenth, scoop up the salt circles and wash them away under a running tap, along with any leftover salt.

If You and Your Twin Soul Are Separated by Distance or Responsibilities

YOU WILL NEED

Fresh or dried culinary bay leaves in a purse ∗ A red candle

TIMING

If you hit a difficult patch in the relationship

THE SPELL

∗ Go to flowing water or the shore. Cast a quarter of the leaves into the water, saying, *Herb of fidelity and eternity, my twin soul love* [Name], *may we connect lastingly.*

∗ Bury another quarter of the leaves on the shoreline/riverbank, saying, *Mother Earth, increase love through the years, so we may be together, and laughter replace tears.*

∗ Scatter another quarter of the leaves into the air, saying, *My twin soul love, my love flies high, reaching yours through the sky.*

∗ Take the rest of the leaves home, burning two leaves in a red candle and say, *Flame and flare, my twin flame, now this fire eternally we share.*

∗ Use the remainder of the bay leaves in cooking.

When an All-Consuming Twin Flame Connection Takes Over Your Life, But Is Not Requited

YOU WILL NEED

A red candle with two wicks ✳ A smaller red candle

TIMING

After a rejection

THE SPELL

✳ Around the base of the double-wicked candle, write invisibly with your dominant hand, IF IN THIS LIFETIME, IT IS MEANT TO BE, TWIN FLAME FLARE IN LOVE FOR ME, OR SET ME FREE.

✳ Light both wicks on this candle, saying, *As this wax melts, let our separate flames join with more intensity, or set me free.*

✳ Light your separate candle, saying, *For I cannot be consumed by love's unrequited fire, come to me in love if you desire, or set me free, that other love can in this lifetime come to me.*

✳ Leave all the candles to burn through and get on with your life, leaving the rest to karma.

When You and Your Twin Flame Have a Burning Shared Ambition or Dream That Means Leaving Familiar Places and People Behind

YOU WILL NEED

Matching beeswax candles on a heatproof tray * A knife
* Small jade crystals * Dried lavender * A piece of green silk

TIMING

During a full moon

THE SPELL

* Light the candles, saying, *This is our dream, our destiny. Others may say we selfish be. But our two flames must join as one, follow our destiny until time is run.*

* When the candles are burned through, draw a circle in the cooling pool of wax between the two, inscribing your entwined initials with a knife and adorning them with crystals.

* Sprinkle lavender outside the circle, saying, [Name any who are pressuring you to stay], *Two flames are we now joined as one, fulfilling our shared purpose, until time is run.*

* Cut out the circle, wrap it in the silk, and keep it as a talisman until you travel.

If Your Twin Soul Proves to Be
Your Soul Enemy

YOU WILL NEED

Scissors ∗ A picture of the two of you on the computer screen ∗ The same picture as a printout ∗ Dark thread tied around the printed picture ∗ An envelope ∗ A black pen

TIMING

During the waning moon

THE SPELL

∗ With the scissors, cut the thread, saying, *Once I loved you desperately, soul twins forever should we be. Now I untangle those ties, no more cruelty, no more lies.*

∗ Onscreen, start to move the figures apart.

∗ Then start to cut the printed-out picture, going from screen to printed-out picture alternately and saying, *First, past connections* [point to screen] *shall go. Then in actuality* [continue cutting], *it shall be so.*

∗ When you have cut the picture in half, seal your ex's picture in the envelope, writing in black on the front RETURN TO KARMA.

∗ Make your ex's picture disappear onscreen, putting yours center screen.

∗ Frame your own picture.

If You Are Constantly Drawn Back to Your Soul Enemy, But S/He Hurts You Each Time

YOU WILL NEED

White paper, which you have divided into squares,
as many or few as you wish, with a black pen
★ Black or blue ink stamps with alphabet letters

TIMING

After another betrayal

THE SPELL

* Fill each square with a stamp of your first initial overstamped with his/hers, saying, *You mesmerize me, overwrite my destiny. Yet this pattern shall be broken. In my life your name shall not be spoken.*

* Go over every square with an X, saying for each, *So I cross you out, in my life you shall not stay. Soul enemy, from this time forward, I wash you clean away.*

* Soak the paper in water and dispose of it.

If You Have a Good Life and a Happy Relationship, and Your Twin Soul Comes Along and Wants You to Go Away Together

YOU WILL NEED

A red candle to the left * An iron pyrite (fool's gold) * A blue candle to the right * A jade crystal

TIMING

Before decision time

THE SPELL

* Light the red candle, putting the fool's gold in front of it, and say, *All that glitters is not gold, though it's lovely to behold.*

* Light the blue candle, placing the jade in front of that, and say, *For promises of future pleasure, should I give up a lifetime's treasure?*

* When you feel ready, extinguish the red candle, saying, *Twin soul, my soul answers your call, but not yet in this lifetime can I sacrifice all.*

* Leave the blue candle to burn through.

* Whisper good-bye in the fool's gold. Keep it in case circumstances change.

* Wear or carry the jade.

If Your Twin Soul Leaves You Forever and You Don't Want to Spend the Rest of Your Life Alone

YOU WILL NEED

A myrrh incense stick ✶ A bowl of dying yellow rose petals
✶ A vanilla incense stick ✶ A bowl of fresh pink petals

TIMING

When the mood strikes

THE SPELL

* Light the myrrh incense behind the yellow petals, saying, *Though my truest love has gone, I do not wish to spend life alone.*

* Light the vanilla incense behind the pink petals, saying, *I know twin love cannot be replaced, but I call to find a loving mate.*

* When the myrrh is burned and cool, scatter the ashes on the dying petals, leaving them outside your property lines.

* When the vanilla is burned and cool, scatter those ashes among the fresh petals, saying, *I call new love and passion too. Soul mate come find me, begin my life anew.*

* Scatter it all just outside your door.

If Everyone Says You Are Foolish
Not to Settle for the Ideal Person
Who Wants to Marry You

Note: There are two versions of this spell. You make the decision which spell to cast or cast both and see how that affects your choice.

Version 1

YOU WILL NEED

Clear quartz crystals or glass nuggets ✳ A map of the world

TIMING

If you want to take a chance

THE SPELL

✳ Scatter your crystals across the map, saying, *Twin soul come to me, over land and over sea. It is for you that I wait, to accept second best I hesitate.*

✳ Gather your crystals, and for each, name a dream or plan you can fulfil with or without a mate.

✳ Now cast them again over the map, saying, *Yet I can change my fate, go out and seek life and my true twin soul. And if, as folks say, s/he may not come, I am in myself complete and whole.*

✳ Choose a crystal and begin a self-dream.

If Everyone Says You Are Foolish Not to Settle for the Ideal Person Who Wants to Marry You

YOU WILL NEED

Two small dolls * A lilac or lily-of-the-valley fragrance
* A green or white candle, if possible with entwined figures

TIMING

If instinct—as well as other people—says to play it safe

THE SPELL

* Anoint the dolls and your own brow, throat, and inner wrist (points for your heart psychic center) each with a single drop of fragrance/essence, saying, *Not in every lifetime, twin soul love does show. But my present soul mate, the flame between our souls may grow.*

* Light the candle repeating the spell.

* Leave the candle to burn through, breathing into it, and between breaths name a shared interest or virtue of your present partner.

* Give the dolls to a child to play with or keep them for your future children.

If You Meet Your Twin Soul Online

YOU WILL NEED

A crystal wand or a smooth stick, pointed at
one end ⋆ Two pictures, one of you and one of
your online love, side by side on the screen

TIMING

Thursday

THE SPELL

* Point your wand toward the screen, saying, *Magick flows through cyberspace, right person, time, and place.*

* Put down the wand, merge the two pictures onscreen, and say, *Technology is a wondrous thing. It doesn't need any fairy wings, to bring my twin soul, my glowing flame. When we meet in person, we shall feel the same.*

* Print out two copies of the new picture, saying, *Twenty years from now, who'll care how we met? The future's ours, and our destiny we'll set.*

* Wave the wand clockwise over the pictures and give your future partner a framed picture of you two together when you meet.

If You Meet Someone Online Who Insists
S/he Is Your Twin Soul, But You Have Doubts

YOU WILL NEED

Three small red jaspers and three green malachites,
set alternately in front of your computer screen
* A blue bag or purse

TIMING

Before going online

THE SPELL

* Touch each crystal left to right, saying, *My handsome prince/fairy princess
  of my dreams, I doubt you are what you seem. Show yourself in your true
  light, then I'll know if you are Mr./Ms. Right.*

* Collect the crystals, shake them six times in your closed, cupped hands,
  and say, *I would know if it was so. My instincts yell, stop, don't go!*

* Set up a meeting in a public place and take your crystals in the bag to
  the meeting.

* Shake them six times before leaving home, saying, *Show yourself in your
  true light. Then I'll know if you are Mr./Ms. Right.*

CHAPTER 2

Attracting Love

I n the previous chapter I wrote of twin soul love. However, some people do not accept the idea of twin souls and past lives, yet, in this lifetime, want to find that faithful, devoted life mate. This chapter focuses on the all-important task of attracting love into your life, whether for a first serious relationship, after hurt, or if you just don't get the chance to meet the right person. The spells help you to find lasting love, first by opening your energy field so that the right kind of partner—not users or losers, who may be drawn to you if you have gentle loving energies—comes into your life and is aware of your charisma and readiness for love.

The spells also call by what some refer to as coincidence or synchronicity—being in the right place at the right time, and totally unexpectedly meeting the right person. Afterward, we may wonder how everything fell into place. This is magick by whatever name you call it; but also, if you lack confidence, your natural love-attracting radar may be subconsciously giving off signals that you are not interested in finding a partner. This can happen if you are naturally shy, have been hurt in love, or your family has always put you down. When you invoke these spells, even if you are seeking to attract a particular person in a spell, if the person is not right for you or for whatever reason chooses not to connect, the love energies will call to you the person who will make you happy.

To Attract Love, Whether Known or Unknown, If You Lack Confidence, Are Shy, or Have Been Hurt

YOU WILL NEED

A mirror ✳ An orange carnelian or amber crystal ✳ Lavender, rose, or ylang-ylang essential oil, diluted in olive oil ✳ A bowl of water to which you have added a few drops of the oil

TIMING

A sunny day

THE SPELL

✳ Gaze into the mirror framed in light. Hold the carnelian to your solar plexus, your inner sun in the center of your upper stomach, saying, *This day I walk into my own light, I bring from within me my own radiance bright. I call the love who is for me right, that we may stay together by day and by night.*

✳ Plunge the carnelian into the water, scattering water drops from it around your hairline.

✳ Do this whenever you go out socially (use the bathroom) or before online dating.

If Your Social Life Is a Disaster or Nil and You Never Get to Meet Any Likely Lovers

YOU WILL NEED

Eight yellow candles, making a square with two
on all four sides ✶ Two blue candles in the middle

TIMING

During a boring night at home

THE SPELL

* Light a single blue candle in the middle, saying, *My love life seriously is in decline, home, work, supermarket, and home again. For a hermit that may be fine. But I'm hardly likely in aisle 5 with the baked beans, to find the one who'll share my dreams.*

* Light the second blue candle in the middle, saying, *OK, so I'm scared of rejection. But on closer inspection, I shall knock down these walls, go into the world and hear love's call.*

* Light the yellow candles, pushing them farther and farther away from the blue ones.

* Leave the candles to burn through. Make plans to join the first of many interest groups on- and offline.

To Become Irresistible on a Special Occasion When Someone You Like a lot Will Be There

YOU WILL NEED

A favorite pendant or necklace * A beautiful flower in a pot

TIMING

Before you get dressed to go out

THE SPELL

* Hold the jewelry a few inches above the flower for a minute or two, saying, *I take your loveliness into me, that my radiance will shine for* [Name] *to see.* [Name], *I ask you dazzled be.*

* Hold the jewelry over the flat, upturned palm of your nondominant hand, then touch your heart with the fingertips of the same hand and put your fingertips to your lips, saying, *Irresistible to all who see, but most of all,* [Name], *be drawn to me.*

* Before you go in to the event, touch your heart with your fingertips, then put your fingertips to your lips, repeating, *Irresistible to all who see, but most of all,* [Name,] *be drawn to me.*

To Attract a Work Colleague Who Seems
Interested But Doesn't Ask You Out

YOU WILL NEED

A coffee, tea, or herbal tea, either made at work
or brought in from a coffee shop ∗ A spoon (use
subtly if you're stirring a take-out drink)

TIMING

Early in the workday

THE SPELL

∗ Stir the drink six times clockwise, saying, *Open your eyes in love to me, gaze on me romantically. For together I know we can be good, just ask me out and you will see.*

∗ Hold the drink between your cupped hands, saying, *Let's go beyond "maybe," "should," and "could" to "will" and "can." As you drink so you shall think, here is my special forever loving wo/man.*

∗ Engineer a touch as you offer the drink. After doing this a couple of mornings, if nothing is forthcoming, suggest meeting for a coffee/drink after work.

Calling the Four Winds to Attract a Yet Unknown Love If There is No One Promising in Your Life

YOU WILL NEED

A long scarf * An open place

TIMING

A windy day

THE SPELL

* When you reach a windy, open place, attach the scarf to the wrist of your dominant hand.

* Turn around in circles, saying, *Boreas of the North, Eurus the East, Notus the South, and the West Zephyrus, I call across land, I call across sea, bring my true love swiftly to me. And if s/he should turn up in the next street, let us with full romance blazing meet.*

* Turn faster until the scarf billows in the wind. Knot it, saying, *Not a user or a loser, not a prince/ss for they're all taken. But one who will my heart awaken.*

* When you get home tie the scarf by one end to a tree or an upstairs window to release the power.

To Attract a Known Love If You Are Both Too Shy to Make the First Move

YOU WILL NEED

Ten small lavender-scented candles in a row

TIMING

Friday evening

THE SPELL

* Light candle 1, saying, *No longer shy.* Light candle 2, saying, *Can't let this love go by.* Light candle 3, saying, *One of us has got to speak.* Light candle 4, saying, *Better be me, mustn't be weak.* Light candle 5, saying, *Showing interest when we greet.* Light candle 6, saying, *One of us, me, suggests we meet.* Light candle 7, saying, *Actually going on a date.* Light candle 8, saying, *Just can't wait.* Light candle 9, saying, *And if s/he does say no.* Light candle 10, saying, *Then on to other love I'll go.*

* Blow out all the candles in reverse order and act. Relight the candles during the following evenings.

Two Deal with a Love Who Is Deliberately Playing Hard to Get

YOU WILL NEED

Three dice * A small bag

TIMING

The beginning of a new week or month

THE SPELL

* Roll the dice, saying, *I'm getting tired of playing games. You're the one who rolls the dice. Keeps me dangling on a string, lovey-dovey, then turns cold. For playing games you're far too old, and I am way too nice.*

* Hold the dice in your cupped hands and shake them, saying, *Now we're playing by my rules. I know you are attracted to me. So treat me respectfully, or someone new I will see.*

* Place the dice in the bag and buy yourself a silver dice charm to wear the next time you see the person.

If You Want Passion and Romance, But Your New Love Interest Is Obsessed with Sports and Hobbies

Version 1

YOU WILL NEED

Olive oil scented with a drop of jasmine oil ★ A red candle
★ A small symbol or silver charm of the hobby
★ A small bowl ★ Masses of flower petals in different colors

TIMING

Before a potentially romantic evening

THE SPELL

* Rub a tiny quantity of oil onto the wax of the unlit candle, upward from the base to the middle and downward from the wick end (not the wick part) to the middle, saying continuously and softly, *Be for me, look at me, for me alone your loving be, romantically, passionately, buried in our love with ecstasy.*

* Put the symbol in the bowl and bury it in petals, repeating the spell words.

* Before your love arrives, scatter some of the petals outdoors. Light the candle as background illumination.

A More Down-to-Earth Version of the Previous Spell to Focus Your New Love's Attention on You and Not More Mundane Interests

Version 2

YOU WILL NEED
Flower petals ∗ Salt ∗ A small bag

TIMING
Before your love arrives

THE SPELL

∗ Scatter a trail of petals from outside your home to the front door, saying, [Name], *me only worship and adore. Don't look over my shoulder for the latest score.*

∗ Put salt in the bag and add some petals, saying, *Sparkle, dazzle, enflame your heart, your body to burn with desire. From when you arrive to when you reluctantly depart, blaze with passionate fire.*

∗ Close the bag with three knots, saying, *I bind, I wind, I find enchantment within. Focusing on me not your game/phone is no sin. I hold your passion here within.*

∗ Put the bag under the mattress and afterward scatter the petals and salt outdoors.

To Find Support If You Live in a Repressive or Very Traditional Society and Your New Love Will Not Be Accepted

YOU WILL NEED

A web of tangled threads on a small hoop ∗ Seeds

TIMING

The end of a month

THE SPELL

∗ Hold the tangle, saying, *Opposition through generations, prejudice that goes back centuries. Yet I will not be tangled in old bitterness. This new love is right for me.*

∗ Gently unravel and unpick the web, saying, *Not trapped by tradition, Encased in convention. This love I shall not abandon, even if I must love secretly, until the day I shall be free, to rejoice in love openly.*

∗ Throw away the untangled web, if possible near an old spiderweb. Scatter seeds, saying, *A new world shall be unfurled. But for now draw to me within the community, those who will support and encourage me.*

If You Want a Lasting Relationship, But Your New Love Is Only Seeking a Fling

YOU WILL NEED

A red candle and a green candle, side by side
* A small bowl of salt

TIMING

At sunset

THE SPELL

* Light the red candle, saying, *Passion you arouse in me, nights we spend in ecstasy. But come the harsh light of day, you kiss me and go away.*

* Light the green candle from the red one, saying, *But I want more, Just so you know the score.*

* Stomp six times with each foot and extinguish the red candle.

* Put salt in the green candle flame, saying, *I want more than a nighttime fling. Show me that you care. Like this candle, flame and flare, not just with lust, but love you must.*

* Relight the red candle and leave both candles to burn through.

If You Are Older and Trying to Get Back in the Dating Game

YOU WILL NEED

Dried lavender ⋆ A photo of your younger self
⋆ Dried sage ⋆ A photo of you now ⋆ A small bag

TIMING

Thursday

THE SPELL

* Scatter some of the lavender on the picture of your youth, saying, *No longer sweet sixteen and never been kissed. That I will miss.*

* Go outside and pour off the lavender, saying, *No regrets, life will yet prove as sweet. But that love I will meet with open eyes, because I am now twice as wise.*

* Scatter some of the sage on the picture of you as you are now and pour that away outdoors.

* Mix the remaining sage and lavender in the bag, saying, *Not too old, For love to unfold, sixteen going on* [add current age]. *Young and wise shall I be, the best combination to love happily.*

* Carry the bag when on a date with someone you met online or in person.

To Attract the Right Online Love

YOU WILL NEED

Your computer or tablet

TIMING

Before visiting a friendship or dating site

THE SPELL

* Switch on the computer, but don't go online.

* Upload a picture of yourself from social media to fill the screen.

* Enchant the image by holding your hands vertically, a few inches from the screen, and moving your dominant hand clockwise and the other hand counterclockwise at the same time. Say softly and continuously, *I call you, love, find me through cyberspace and time, the one true love who will be mine.*

* Go online, repeating the spell words faster and faster. When you can say the words no more, stand up, bring your arms backward, then forward, make a clap over your head, and sit down fast. Connect with the site or name that is in front of you.

For a First Love

Heart-shaped candies, set in a heart shape around a
pink candle, at left ✳ A green candle, at right

TIMING

Early Friday

THE SPELL

✳ Light the pink candle to the left, saying, *First love they say is sweetest.
I call you love to awaken my heart. I will offer my devotion, and ask that
we never part.*

✳ Light the green candle from the pink one, saying, *Wherever you are,
first love, near or far, may these lights of love guide you to me* [blow softly
in each flame] *and me to you, my lover true.*

✳ Eat two candies, saying, *This candy I eat, and when we meet, that love
shall be forever sweet.*

✳ Repeat the spells on different days until all the candies are eaten.

To Rebuild Trust in a New Love
after Being Badly Hurt

YOU WILL NEED

A half-full vacuum cleaner bag ✳ Lavender heads or
a lavender-based powdered carpet cleaner

TIMING

Sunday

THE SPELL

✳ Empty the vacuum bag into the garbage, saying, *Ashes to ashes, dust to dust, gone is that bad love, restored shall be trust.*

✳ Scatter lavender across the floor and then vacuum it up, saying, *The flowers of love shall blossom again, joy replacing redundant pain. It is not the past for which I yearn, but for new love and trust reborn.*

✳ Go out to a new place, or if you have met someone, make an arrangement to see each other.

CHAPTER 3

Increasing Commitment, Encouraging Marriage, OR Building A Relationship BY Permanently Living Together

nce you have found the right person, the next stage is to deepen your commitment to that relationship. Informal commitment ceremonies are increasingly celebrated by couples, oftentimes with friends and family present. However, if your partner shows you by her/his actions that s/he wants to spend the rest of her/his life with you, but doesn't want a formal announcement, you can, either alone or with your partner, use spells in this chapter to mark the beginning of the next major phase in your relationship.

Of course, there can be all kinds of complications in moving from a casual relationship to lasting commitment, especially if one partner has previously been badly hurt in love or one or both of you isn't yet free.

This chapter therefore offers spells to help overcome obstacles to lasting love, increase commitment, and also various ways of marking togetherness, whether celebrating moving in together or an informal alternative, or in addition to a more formal commitment ceremony, such as a handfasting or a wedding.

For a Lover Who Says All the Right Things But Won't Commit

YOU WILL NEED

A basket of leaves ∗ Coriander seeds
∗ A wide-necked flask of water

TIMING

During the crescent moon

THE SPELL

∗ Outdoors scatter half the leaves, saying, *You don't commit and time goes by. Your words are loving, but your actions love denies.*

∗ Plant half the seeds, saying, *Seeds, once planted, the roots go deep. I want you with me when I wake and sleep, when I'm scintillating or have a cold, stay with me as I grow old.*

∗ Mix the rest of the seeds with the leaves. Pour them into the flask, swirl it around, and say, *Commit to me, show me you care. Prove to me you'll always be there.*

∗ Pour the contents of the flask into running water, saying, *Demonstrate you love me, as rivers flow. Real commitment to me show.*

If You Have Talked about Getting Engaged or Married and Want to Set a Definite Date

YOU WILL NEED

A ring that fits your wedding finger ∗ A sheet calendar with squares, flat on the table ∗ A hole punch ∗ A green ribbon

TIMING

When you want a definite date, but your partner is hesitating

THE SPELL

∗ Place the ring on the date when you would like the engagement or wedding to take place, saying, *With this ring, I do not you bind, but fix a date when you will find, me waiting the whole world to show, we are joined in heart and soul and mind.*

∗ Make two holes in your chosen date, thread the ribbon through them, and knot it tightly in back.

∗ Cut out the square, keeping it in your bedside drawer.

∗ Propose/set the wedding day.

∗ Wear the ring on a new ribbon around your neck on your engagement/ wedding day.

To Bring Good Luck When Moving in Together for the First Time

YOU WILL NEED

A small box ⋆ Four small items, placed in the box: something old, something new, something borrowed, something blue ⋆ Four blue candles

TIMING

As soon as you arrive

THE SPELL

* Carry your box through the front door and, if there is a back door, out of that and in again, ending in the center of your new home, saying, *May good luck enter and never depart. May health, prosperity dwell here and above all loving hearts.*

* Put the box on a table, surrounding it with four candles, one near each corner. Light each one clockwise, repeating the spell words four times.

* When the candles are burned through, put the old item in the most northern corner, the new one in the east, the borrowed one in the south, and the blue one in the west, repeating the spell words as you set each one.

If You Have a Long-Distance Relationship Because One of You Lives or Works Overseas

YOU WILL NEED

Solar lights (or small battery powered candles)

TIMING

As darkness falls

THE SPELL

* Set solar lights (or small battery powered candles) from the front door to the front of your property. If you have no outdoor space, set from your front door to the center of your house

* When your solar lights come on (or switch on your battery-powered candles), walk from beginning to end, saying, *True love is not limited by miles. It spans oceans, forests, and through skies. Across the distance the light of love calls, we are not far away at all.*

* Stand in the middle of the light path, reaching out your hands and arms. Turn in all directions, saying, *Though my heart does daily for you yearn, I commit my life to you, my distance love, until the day you/I can return.*

To Make a Commitment of the Heart If You Cannot Be Together Openly

YOU WILL NEED

Two beeswax candles in flat holders, one on each end of the table ⁕ Two mimosa incense sticks, one on each end of the table ⁕ A bowl of sand ⁕ A knife or letter opener ⁕ A small bag

TIMING

Sunday

THE SPELL

⁕ Light both candles, first left, then right, saying, *Life not love keeps us apart. We are joined in souls, minds, and hearts.*

⁕ Light each incense stick from its neighboring candle. Holding an incense stick in each hand, make a smoke bridge between the candles and say, *Break through the blocks of secrecy, that we may share love openly.*

⁕ Plunge both incense sticks into the sand, lighted end down.

⁕ Cut a figure in the pool of cooling wax beneath each candle.

⁕ Keep the figures in a small bag. Each week hold the bag, saying, *Our hearts we have pledged eternally. I call you closer, come to me.*

When You Have Been Together a Long Time, but the Mention of Marriage Hits a Brick Wall

YOU WILL NEED

An ivy leaf for every year you've been together
★ A bowl of water ★ Two silver rings
★ A frond of trailing ivy ★ A small bag

TIMING

Thursday

THE SPELL

* Cast the ivy leaves into the water, saying, *Ivy, ivy I love you. Bring me marriage true. I have waited so very long. Make him/her want me too.*

* Tie the rings together with the ivy frond, floating them in the water and say, *Round and round the circle turns, love that never ends. With these rings do we wed. Marry me soon, my lover, protector, and best friend.*

* Untie the rings; when dry, put them in the bag under your mattress.

* Cast the ivy leaves and the ivy frond into fast-running water, calling, *Marry me soon, my lover, protector, and best friend.*

If You Need Your Lover to Break a Connection with an Ex That Stands between You and 100 Percent Commitment

YOU WILL NEED

A bag containing dried lentils or beans ✳ A red candle in a
pot of soil ✳ A strong red thread with three knots, one in the
middle and one at either end ✳ An unknotted blue cord

TIMING

After interference

THE SPELL

✳ Shaking the bag vigorously ten times, say ten times, *You,* [name partner],
*procrastinate, hesitate, tread on eggshells not to offend. But no longer,
this interference has to end.*

✳ Light the candle, take out the knotted red cord, burn the central knot
in the flame, and drop the broken cord in the soil, saying, *Three in
this love henceforward shall only be two, me and you.*

✳ Put the blue cord in the bag, shake the bag ten times, and say ten times,
You and me, only, my love shall you be.

✳ Blow out the candle.

A Vanilla or Yarrow Commitment Spell after a Marriage Ceremony

YOU WILL NEED

Dried vanilla powder ∗ Dried yarrow leaves or flowers
(you can use split tea bags) ∗ A bowl and a wooden
spoon ∗ A small purse with a drawstring

TIMING

After your honeymoon

THE SPELL

∗ Mix the vanilla and yarrow very gently in the bowl, saying seven times slowly and quietly, *Seven years they say, fidelity, seven and seven times more until infinity. This is your vow to me, my pledge to you, to love each other eternally, our whole life through.*

∗ Put the mix in the bag, repeating the spell words and tie the drawstring with seven knots.

∗ Hang it over your bed and replace it every seven years, or if you prefer, when the fragrance fades.

A Candle Joining Commitment Spell

One large white candle with two wicks * Two smaller
white candles, set on either side of the larger candle

TIMING

During the waxing moon

THE SPELL

* Light the small candle at left, saying, *My love, I offer my heart to you, love everlasting, love so true. I light this flame, in love's own name.*

* Light the small candle at right, saying, *My love, I ask that we will be, eternally united in love and fidelity.*

* Light the left-hand wick on the central candle with the flame of the left-hand candle, saying, *No more two but one, may our love last so long as the sun shines, and the waters of earth run.*

* Light the second wick from the right-hand candle, repeating the same spell words.

* Blow out the candle at left and then the candle at right, saying, *Together forever, no longer alone, drawing strength from being one.*

* Leave the large candle to burn through.

A Plant Joining Commitment Spell

Two trailing plants * Red, green, yellow,
blue, and orange ribbons

TIMING

During the first moon quarter

THE SPELL

* Plant the two trailing plants very close in the ground or in a large
  planter, saying, *May our love through the years grow close and naturally.
  May our roots entwine, not stiflingly, but willingly.*

* Join two or three fronds from each, saying, *I reach out to you and
  you reach out to me. I offer to you and you offer to me, love, trust,
  and lasting fidelity.*

* Tie on each plant a red ribbon for passion, a green ribbon for trust, a
  yellow ribbon for lasting joy, a blue ribbon for fidelity, and an orange
  ribbon for unity, saying as a soft continuous chant, *Passion grows, trust
  knows. Fidelity and joy will through months and years increase, creating
  unity, so our growing love through our whole life shall be.*

58

A Sand Joining Commitment Spell

Two spoons ✳ Two jars of different-colored sands,
one for each of you ✳ An ornamental glass
vase ✳ A selection of small crystals

TIMING

During the crescent moon

THE SPELL

✳ Spoon a layer of colored sand into the bottom of the vase from your jar, saying, *This pledge I make as long as the sands of time do run, that we will live in unity forever under the sun.*

✳ Next, put in the vase a layer of sand for your partner from the second jar, repeating the spell words.

✳ Continue placing alternating layers of sand in the vase. When the vase is almost full, add a layer of crystals, naming for each one a quality you value in your partner and what you offer, saying, *Mingled and mixed, forever fixed. Like grains of sand, none will ever break us apart, for we are one unity, one love, one heart.*

✳ Keep the vase in your joint home.

A Handfasting Commitment Spell
for Making or Renewing Vows

YOU WILL NEED

A dish of salt ⋆ A dish of water ⋆ Two red cords ⋆ Two wedding
rings, silver or gold ⋆ Dried rosemary or vanilla pods ⋆ A small fire
pit or a large candle in the middle of a large circle of petals, large
enough to walk around ⋆ Two small white candles on either side of
a large one ⋆ A broom on the ground, close to the table/ fire pit
inside the circle, used to hold the items ⋆ A bouquet ⋆ Rose petals

TIMING

*Outdoors, any day in natural beauty or a family garden,
large enough for the two of you plus your guests*

THE SPELL

* Pour salt into the dish of water, which your partner holds. Have your partner
  swirl the water and sprinkle a little on the cords, tying them together, while
  both of you say together, *So willingly, do we join our lives, throughout eternity.*

* Have both of you cast rosemary on the fire, saying, *May our love always burn
  bright.* Exchange promises and silver or gold rings.

* Both of you now light and join your separate candle flames in the larger
  central candle, saying, *Now we two are one.*

* Tie your right hand to your partner's right hand with the tied red cords,
  saying, *Those whom the God/Goddess/the Power of Light has joined together in
  their hearts, may none set apart.*

* Kiss each other, jump over the broom, tossing the bouquet as you run out of
  the circle and as guests scatter the petals. Leave the candles burning.

A Handfasting That Isn't an Actual Ceremony

YOU WILL NEED

Two small figures, made from wax by melting two beeswax candles
on a heatproof tray and cutting them out before the spell
* Seven ribbons of gold and seven of silver, and silver and gold
thread for attaching * A tiny straw hoop or basket * Seven
flower heads on small stems in red, yellow, and orange

TIMING

When the sun and moon are both in the sky

THE SPELL

* Attach the figures face-to-face with ribbons/thread in seven knots,
  to the hoop/basket, saying, *Handfast, dear heart, never to part.*

* Next, attach the flowers with thread to the hoop/basket, each
  with seven knots, saying, *Hand bind, love wind, to find, freedom
  in unity, love vows made willingly, forever to be.*

* Add the remaining ribbons.

* Sail your hoop/basket on water, saying, *Together, forever.*

A Traditional Ring Joining Rite for Commitment

YOU WILL NEED

Two copper rings ✳ A circle of white paper under
the rings ✳ Dried mixed parsley, sage,
rosemary, and thyme ✳ A red pen

TIMING

Thursday

THE SPELL

✳ On the paper around the rings, draw as a circle an image of clasped
hands, followed by entwined hearts, followed by a knot, followed
by clasped hands again, continuing until you have completely
encircled the rings.

✳ Scatter the herb mix around the circle, saying, *Parsley, sage, rosemary,
thyme, make this love forever mine.*

✳ Moving your dominant hand clockwise and your nondominant hand
counterclockwise, palms facing down, a few inches above the rings,
say, *Our hands and hearts with one consent, have tied this knot till
death prevent.*

✳ Go around the circle clockwise, touching each symbol as you repeat
the rhyme.

✳ Keep the rings together with the folded paper until your wedding day.

The Flowing Waters Commitment Spell

Two small jugs of water ⋆ Seven white flowering
plants in small pots ⋆ A large empty jug

TIMING

On a full moon night

THE SPELL

* Leave the small water jugs outdoors on a full moon night, surrounded by the plants.

* In the morning, place the large jug on the ground.

* Taking a small jug in each hand, carefully pour water into the larger jug, saying, *The waters of love, join together. Which is mine, which is yours, no one shall ever know. But the waters of our commitment as one henceforward* will flow.

* When the smaller jugs are empty, pour water on each of the flowering plants, saying, *Like these flowers through weeks, months, hours, our love will grow in sunshine and through showers.*

* Plant your flowers in a large pot or outdoors. Each day for a week, water them with the moon water you made.

CHAPTER 4

Spells TO Encourage Passion IN Love AND Deter Destructive Lust

As you make love, whether for the first time, with a new partner, or within a relationship of many years, you share in the tradition of sacred marriage that dates back thousands of years. The sacred marriage is one that permeates all cultures, representing the union of male and female.

These spells focus on passion, from encouraging a first meaningful sexual encounter with someone new to reviving passion in a longer-term relationship. In everyday life, passion sometimes takes second place to worldly concerns. By the same token, a burning passion—for example, at work for your boss who is not available, or for a married neighbor—can cause huge disruption. You will find spells in the chapter on overcoming temptation.

Sexual predators and abusive partners can make you feel violated and destroy your self-esteem. You need earthly support to escape the situation, but anti-passion spells can deter someone who is making your life hell, whether by groping or by constant inappropriate remarks.

Finally, sexual demons—male incubi and female succubi—have been a problem for hundreds of years, especially for people in their late teens, twenties, and thirties. They attack at night, when the victim is in a semiconscious state between sleep and waking, lying on top of the victim and suffocating her/him. It is a problem commonly encountered and for which I am frequently asked to cast spells. One is included in this chapter.

A Naughty Ice-Cream Spell to Seduce an Unawakened Lover

YOU WILL NEED

An ice-cream cone

TIMING

Before you meet

THE SPELL

* Begin to slowly lick the ice cream while rubbing your fingers slowly up and down the cone to catch any drips.

* Stop licking and say slowly, *Awaken passion, arouse burning desire. Seduce me, totally surrender, irresistibly be consumed by lust's fire.*

* Continue licking, catching the drips, and saying the spell words, slowly and sensually, rubbing the cone and repeating the spell words.

* When the ice cream is gone, say, *You have no power to turn away, take me passionately, completely, you are totally under my sway.*

* Share ice cream when you meet.

To Increase Passion If You Have Been Together a While

YOU WILL NEED

An entwined red beeswax lovers' candle ∗ Pure olive oil with a drop of ylang-ylang or jasmine oil added ∗ Four musk incense cones, one in each corner of the bedroom ∗ Nine hairs from you and from a hairbrush, plus nine of your partner's

TIMING

Before s/he arrives

THE SPELL

∗ On one of the figures on the candle, using the nail of the index finger on your dominant hand, scratch the word FLAME and on the other FLARE.

∗ Stroke each figure on the entwined candle in turn, from base to center and from tip (not too close to the wick) with pure olive oil with a drop of ylang-ylang or jasmine oil added, saying slowly, *Passion grows, wax flows. In ecstasy, burn with desire for me.*

∗ Light the incense. When burned and cool, mix the incense ash with the hairs. Scatter them outdoors.

∗ Light the candle in the bedroom before lovemaking.

Before Lovemaking for the First Time or with a New Partner

YOU WILL NEED

Four floral-scented candles ✶ Rose or lavender essential oil, diluted in slightly warmed almond or olive oil

TIMING

Before your lover arrives

THE SPELL

* Light a candle in each corner of the room.

* Anoint with oil your root chakra energy center, saying softly, *I am the earth, passion pulsate.*

* Anoint with oil your sacral chakra, saying, *I am the moon, desire radiate within me increasingly.*

* Anoint with oil your solar plexus chakra, saying, *I am pure fire, enflame me with passionate intensity.*

* Anoint with oil your heart chakra, saying, *I am the winds, soaring to ever-greater delight.*

* Anoint with oil your throat chakra, saying, *I am pure sound, resounding continuously as growing ecstasy.*

* Anoint with oil your brow chakra, saying, *I am pure light, moving beyond time, our bodies shall entwine.*

* Finally, anoint with oil your crown chakra, saying, *No longer two, but one.*

CROWN
BROW
THROAT
HEART
SOLAR
SACRAL
ROOT

A Quickie Passion Inducer
If the Kids Are Out

YOU WILL NEED

Salt ∗ A musk incense stick ∗ A red candle
∗ A bowl of rose fragrance

THE SPELL

∗ Decide in advance where you will make love; the sofa, the kitchen table, or the bed.

∗ Scatter a circle of salt around the site of your lovemaking, saying, *I call my love with the power of the earth. Passion, lust find rebirth— and quickly.*

∗ Circle the site of your lovemaking with the lighted stick of incense, saying, *I call my love with the power of air, ecstasy, and the old G spots revive in me there.*

∗ Circle the site of your lovemaking with the lighted candle, saying, *I call my love with the power of fire, restore between us our old desire. Once kindled in moments behind the shed, prove that passion isn't dead.*

∗ Finally, sprinkle a circle of rose water around the site of your love-making, saying, *I call my love with water power. Let us see stars in less than an hour.*

A More Leisurely Earth, Air, Fire, and Water Spell to Maintain or Restore Passion in a Relationship

YOU WILL NEED

A red candle ✳ Any spice incense stick ✳ Rose petals
✳ A bowl of water with a drop or two of rose oil added

TIMING

After dusk

THE SPELL

✳ Light the candle and incense.

✳ Starting at the headboard, scatter a circle of rose petals clockwise around the bed, then spiral your incense, the candle, and finally the rose water, chanting softly and slowly, *Earth, air, water, fire, make him/her passionately me desire.*

✳ Sit in the center of the bed, making circles a few inches above the bed, hands palms down, the right circling clockwise and the left counterclockwise, repeating the spell words.

✳ When you can chant no faster, clap your hands, saying, *Earth, air, water, fire, bring I ask this night desire.*

✳ Blow out the candle, saying, *Passion be, the power I free.*

✳ Leave the incense burning.

A Fragrance to Make You Irresistible
If Your Partner Has a Lower Libido Than Yours

YOU WILL NEED

A silver candle ✳ His favorite fragrance and yours in two
separate dishes ✳ Two small clay or worry dolls

TIMING

During the full moon

THE SPELL

* Light the candle and set your fragrances so that the light shines on
  them, saying, *Fragrance, be filled with light, that irresistible may I be
  in his/her sight. Power of fire increase for me his/her desire.*

* Anoint your and your partner's dolls around the root chakra
  (see diagram on page 69), repeating the spell words.

* Mix the fragrances, anoint your inner wrist points and then the corners
  of the bed sheets, saying the spell words again.

* Leave the candle and incense to burn through. Before lovemaking,
  anoint the headboard with the mixed fragrances.

* Cast the dolls into running water.

To Draw an Overworked or Overstressed Partner to Your Bed

YOU WILL NEED:

A large red pillar candle ✳ Strawberry or any
fruit incense stick ✳ Rose petals

TIMING

10 P.M.

THE SPELL

✳ Light the candle and incense, saying, *Candle of love, incense of desire,
I call my love in fragrance and in fire. In fire and in fragrance, be drawn
to me. Totally enraptured, captured be.*

✳ Taking a handful of rose petals, pass your closed hands three times
around the flame and three times through the incense smoke, saying,
*In flower, fragrance and in fire, three times my love I call with desire.
One to remind, two to bind, three with passion to entwine.*

✳ Scatter all the rose petals in a clockwise circle around the candle
and incense.

✳ Blow out the candle and let the incense burn through. Scoop up some
of the rose petals and hide them beneath the mattress.

A Ritual for Combining Passion with Tenderness If Your Partner is a Wham–Bam–Thank You Ma'am—or Sir—Lover

YOU WILL NEED

A gentle love incense, such as jasmine or mimosa
* A red candle for passion * Bubble bath * Olive
oil * A gentle lavender love fragrance for the bath,
to which is added five drops of ylang-ylang oil

TIMING

Before lovemaking

THE SPELL

* Light the incense in your bathroom, saying softly, *Incense flow, passion grow. But tenderness show, it shall be so.*

* Stroke the unlit candle, with oil, working from the base to the center and from the top to the center, saying, *Candle glow, wax flow, passion grow. It shall be so.*

* Light the candle.

* Run your bath, combining gentle fragrance and ylang-ylang oil. In the water, massage yourself with the bubbles, repeating the incense and the candle chant.

* Afterward, take the candle and the incense back to the bedroom, calling your partner through the candle flame.

To Alleviate Male Sexual Dysfunction

Frankincense or orange essential oil ★ Sunflower oil
★ A small dish ★ A pointed lodestone or hematite crystal

TIMING

Twelve hours or more before lovemaking

THE SPELL

* Add a few drops of frankincense or orange essential oil to the dish of sunflower oil and soak the lodestone/hematite in the dish, from when you awaken until noon, saying as you add it, *Sun power, at this hour, fill me with potency and virility. Fulfilled and fulfilling in passion shall I be.*

* Repeat the spell words as you turn the lodestone over at noon.

* Leave it in the dish until dusk.

* At dusk, rinse and dry the lodestone well, holding it in your dominant hand.

* Touch your genitals with it, repeating the spell words, and do this again before lovemaking.

85

To Alleviate Female Sexual Dysfunction

YOU WILL NEED

Scented tea lights ∗ Lavender- or rose-scented soap ∗ A metal nail file ∗ Lavender essential oil ∗ Rose essential oil ∗ Olive oil

TIMING

Before your lover arrives

THE SPELL

∗ Run a bath, with tea lights illuminating the bathroom.

∗ Etch into the soap with the metal nail file the words PASSION on one side and ECSTASY on the other.

∗ Add five drops of lavender oil and five drops of rose oil to the water, saying, *Sensuality and passion flow into me. Radiant I am and radiant shall I be, for the one who waits for me. Fears and inhibitions, go from me.*

∗ In the bath, massage your thighs and breasts with the soap, repeating the spell words.

∗ When you have finished your bath, massage yourself with lavender and rose oil, diluted in warm olive oil, saying, *Fears and inhibitions have flowed from me. I open myself to joy and ecstasy.*

∗ Keep the soap, renewing the etched words as needed.

To Deal with a Male Sexual Predator in the Workplace or in Your Personal Life

YOU WILL NEED

A phallic-shaped crystal or stone, or a teaspoon

TIMING

On the approach of the predatory male

THE SPELL

* Vigorously twist the crystal, stone, or spoon three times counterclockwise between your hands, saying in your head three times, *Feel the discomfort of your lechery, every time you approach me. You will recall how painful it can be.*

* When the predator has gone, wash the crystal/spoon under hot water and then plunge it into ice-cold water, saying, *The fires of inappropriate lust be cooled, feel them diminish. You appear not a daring predator, but a fool.*

To Deal with a Female Sexual Predator in the Workplace or in Your Personal Life

YOU WILL NEED

An ammonite or spiral-shaped shell ★ A very small drawstring bag

TIMING

Whenever you feel intimidated

THE SPELL

* Cupping your hands firmly around the shell, say in your head nine times, *Back off, subtlety you seriously do lack. Your unwanted intimacy is not welcome to me. I send it back.*

* Press hard into the shell, saying, *Harder and harder do I press. This message on you, I shall impress.*

* Toss the shell and catch it, closing your hands around it, and say, *Bound, no reason found, for you to intimidate me again. Know the pain.*

* Press the shell hard a final time and shut it in a tightly knotted bag where it is an extremely tight fit until needed again.

To Deal with Sexual Abuse When You Are Getting No Help

A purple candle * A long pin, like a hat pin

TIMING

After dark

THE SPELL

* Light the candle, allowing the wax to begin to melt, and say, *So burns away your evil desire,* [Name], *your abuse I banish in candle fire.*

* As the wax melts, stick the pin a third of the way down the candle, so that it penetrates the wick within. Say, *It is not this pin I wish to burn, but you* [Name], *from your viciousness turn. Into the candle flame, bend, pin, bend and evil end.*

* When the pin falls from the candle, say, *Fall, pin, fall. Let my life be free from this evil thrall. Burn candle all.*

* Extinguish the candle and dispose of the wax and the pin.

To Remove an Incubus (Male) or a Succubus (Female) Sexual Demon Who Attacks While You Sleep

YOU WILL NEED

A red candle ∗ Dried nettles (or use two split nettle tea bags) ∗ A wide-necked bottle with a lid ∗ A small piece of a thorn ∗ Vinegar

TIMING

Before you go to sleep

THE SPELL

∗ Light the candle. Put nettles in the bottom of the bottle, then push in the thorn, saying, *Vile demon, enter here. Me, you shall no longer attack. From where you came, I send you back.*

∗ Pour in vinegar to cover the thorn. Leave the bottle open and blow out the candle.

∗ Put your hands around the outside of the bottle, saying, *Within this spirit trap, I lure you in. You are unable to resist, and trapped within, You shall remain, feeling your self-inflicted pain.*

∗ The next morning, put the lid on the bottle.

∗ Throw the bottle in the garbage away from your home.

If You're Ready to Take a Chance on What May Be Just One Night of Passion with the Boss or Office High Jinks with a Colleague or at an Office Party

YOU WILL NEED

Ten red tea lights in a row

TIMING

When tempted

THE SPELL

* Light the candles left to right fast, saying fast, *I know the score, but definitely do want more.* [Name], *you excite me, you delight me. I run unhesitatingly through temptation's door.*

* Blow the candles out equally fast, saying, *10, 9, 8, 7, 6, 5, 4, 3, 2, 1, passion come.*

* Relight the candles, saying, *Who knows what the results may be, from this instant passion, long-lasting love may come to me. But what the heck, I'll act and see.*

* Keep lighting and blowing out the candles and on the tenth lighting, leave them to burn through.

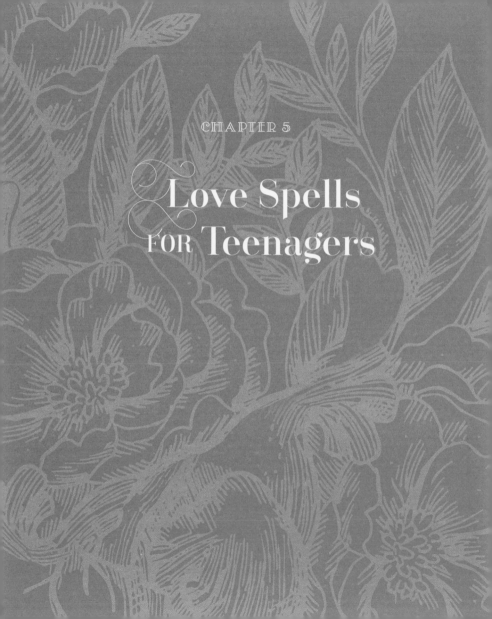

CHAPTER 5

Love Spells
FOR Teenagers

First love may last forever, and those who meet in the teenage years do sometimes remain together for a lifetime. But first love or a love that does not last may be painful. Younger people have to deal with a new and bittersweet yet deep love connection with another person that may dominate every waking and sleeping moment. At the same time, they may be struggling with issues of personal identity, study, or a first job; confidence; and friendships that may conflict with the new exclusive love relationship, giving rise to jealousy because friends feel neglected. Parents, themselves in their middle years and undergoing changes, are suddenly faced with their son or daughter experiencing love with a person of whom they may not approve. Social media puts love or lack of love under the global microscope, and exes or bitchy schoolmates may use it to cause trouble. Flirtations or an intense love suddenly cooling for no apparent reason can cause great unhappiness. Though there are teenage spells in other chapters, this chapter focuses on many of the issues connected with teenage love, and offers spells to help resolve problems and make the early years of loving happy and fulfilling.

If You Fall in Love, but the Other Person Isn't Responding

85

YOU WILL NEED

A pastry bag, filled with ready-made icing for piping
* Heart-shaped or circular-shaped cookies,
store-bought or homemade

TIMING

Any morning at home

THE SPELL

* On day 1, in icing, pipe the name of the person you desire on the cookie, and say, *In sweetness do I call you. Notice me, that you may be mine, madly and passionately, for the whole world to see.*

* Eat the cookie and repeat the spell words.

* On day 2, draw a heart in icing on the cookie, repeat the spell words, and eat the cookie.

* On day 3, place your initials within a heart on the cookie, say the spell words again, and eat the cookie.

* As soon as possible, offer your love a cookie, and, as you hand it over, brush his/her hand and say the spell words in your mind.

If Your Best Friend Is Jealous of or Wants Your Partner for His/Her Own and Is Trying to Break up Your Relationship

YOU WILL NEED

A deep bowl of sugar
* A thin-bladed knife or letter opener

THE SPELL

* Draw an eye in the sugar with the knife to represent the eye of envy (it does not matter if it disappears).

* Say as you draw it, *Best friend, This jealousy must end. Your envy divides you from me. Though I love you, my lover I must choose, and so best friend, you will lose.*

* Dissolve the sugar under a running tap, saying, *Your eye of envy no more troubles me. To your old sweetness please go back, or my friendship you will lack.*

* Do something nice for your best friend.

If Everyone Else but You Has a Date for the Prom or a Special Occasion

YOU WILL NEED
A mirror ✴ Six tea lights or small white candles,
set along the edge of the mirror

TIMING
After dark

THE SPELL

* Put on your prettiest frock or smartest outfit and carefully, so you don't burn yourself or your clothes, light the candles left to right, saying, *All dressed up, nowhere to go, a gorgeous gal/guy like me, it can't be so. I call your name in candle flame* [name desired person]. *Ask me to be your date. Don't hesitate, I can't wait.*

* Blow out the candles, relight them, and repeat the spell words.

* Do this ten more times (making eleven lightings in all). On the last lighting, say, *Love, now hear me through candle flame. Invite me to* [name event] *as I call your name.*

* Leave the candles to burn through.

If, After a First Date, Your New Love Hasn't Contacted You or Responded to Your Calls or Texts

YOU WILL NEED

Your phone

TIMING

When you know the person will be free

THE SPELL

* Either write a text or have the number ready to dial, but do not connect.

* Hold the phone between your hands, then place it next to your heart, then hold the screen to your lips.

* Now, holding the phone in your nondominant hand, pass the other hand in clockwise circles a few inches above the phone, saying, softly and slowly, *Don't want flowers or a letter. The first date was good, the second better. Call me, text, whatever's best. Let's leave fate to decide the rest.*

* Call or send the text, saying as you do, *Message send, this silence end. Love can be sweet, so please let's meet.*

If You Are Going on a First Date with Someone Special

YOU WILL NEED

A jasmine or mimosa incense stick and an incense holder * A bottle of your favorite fragrance

TIMING

While getting ready

THE SPELL

* Light the incense. Make smoke spirals holding the incense stick like a pen, seven times clockwise around the fragrance bottle, saying seven times, *I am pure fragrance, I am pure light,* [name the person you wish to enchant]. *I will dazzle you this night.*

* Return the incense to the holder.

* Pass both hands over the fragrance bottle seven times, your dominant hand clockwise and the other counterclockwise, at the same time, repeating the spell words seven times.

* Put a drop of fragrance on your ankle bones, your knees, your wrists, at the base of your throat, at the center of your brow, and on your hairline, saying the spell words again.

* Finally, place a drop on a tissue or handkerchief and take it with you.

* Let the incense burn away.

To Turn Your Beastly Boyfriend into a Handsome Prince

YOU WILL NEED

A model Beast from Disney's *Beauty and the Beast*®
★ A green ribbon or piece of cord

TIMING

Wednesday

THE SPELL

* Shake your model Beast saying, *Belle turned her Beast into a gorgeous prince. You are harder work. I want roses, chocolates, romantic words. Baseball, soccer, pin-up chicks, Is all I've ever heard.*

* Hang your Beast with the ribbon by one of its feet from your bedroom wall for seven days, shaking it as you pass and saying, *Hanging on in hope of attention, but soccer scores are all you mention. As for your roving eye, well hardly a day without that goes by.*

* On day 8, move the ribbon from the Beast's foot to around the Beast's neck, saying, *On a leash, I'll keep you tight, till the day you start to treat me right.*

* Leave your Beast dangling until he improves.

To Turn Your Beast into a Beauty

YOU WILL NEED

A small basket * A big box of individually wrapped, heart-shaped candies * Rose petals * A model of Belle from Disney's *Beauty and the Beast* or a fairy princess doll * A small piece of jewelry

TIMING

When she has stood you up again in favor of her friends

THE SPELL

* Fill the basket with candy, saying, *Always texting and phoning your friends, carrying your bags through shops, never ends. Bitching and twitching if I see my mates, fluttering your lashes at other guys, I hate.*

* Put rose petals in the center of the basket and rest the doll on them, saying, *Sweeter be, toward me. Make me the center of your attention. Right now I hardly get a mention. I love you and you love me, so don't be beastly, be my Beauty.*

* After 24 hours, add a small piece of jewelry and give the basket to your girl.

If You Are Attracted to Someone But Are Too Shy to Let Her/Him Know

YOU WILL NEED

A selfie of yourself hiding your face, on the screen of your computer ★ A second selfie of yourself smiling on a second screen ★ Yellow ribbons

TIMING

Before you know you will meet

THE SPELL

* Look at the picture of yourself on the screen hiding your face and say, *I am shy, don't know why. I know you* [Name] *like me, need to let you see, I'd like to get to know you, show what fun I can be.*

* Delete the image.

* Frame the picture of yourself smiling with a bright border on the second screen, saying, *Little Ms./Mr. Shyness has gone away. The confident new Mr./Ms. is here to stay.*

* Print out the smiling picture and hang it in your room, surrounded by yellow ribbons.

* Put one of the ribbons in your phone case when next you meet.

If Your Boyfriend or Girlfriend Is Flirting with Others on Social Media or in Everyday Life

YOU WILL NEED

A red candle ✷ An old spoon
✷ A blue candle ✷ Salt

TIMING

Tuesday

THE SPELL

✷ Hold the red unlit candle, saying, *Only me, fill your mind and fill your heart. Your flirting is driving us apart.*

✷ Light the red candle, saying, *You have promised me devotion. I know you mean to be true. But this dangerous game, like this flame, will burn our love right through.*

✷ Extinguish the candle with the spoon.

✷ Light the blue candle, saying, *Turn red to blue, temptation to love true. Don't destroy what is so precious, between me and you.*

✷ Put salt in the flame, saying, *Burn long, take away this wrong. I will to you faithful be, but only if you show me loyalty.*

✷ Leave the blue candle to burn through.

If You Argue and S/He Storms Off and Won't Answer Your Calls or Texts

YOU WILL NEED

Your phone

TIMING

When you have been ignored again

THE SPELL

* Call up the number, but don't phone or text it.

* Stare at the screen and say louder and louder in your mind, *Call me, text me, must respond, been too long. Doesn't matter who was right or wrong. Text or call now, we can fix all. Just text or call, anyway, anyhow.*

* Take the number off the screen and repeat the spell words and actions ten times in all.

* Put the number up for the eleventh time, send a conciliatory text, and then go out and do something fun with friends.

If You Are in Love with a Movie Star or Celebrity

YOU WILL NEED

A picture of the celebrity, including, if possible, an
autograph or signature (found online) ★ A gold
candle ★ Twelve small, clear, quartz crystals

TIMING

Three days, starting on Sunday

THE SPELL

* Hold the picture, light the candle, and say, *Ordinary folks marry prince/
  sses. Celebrities fall in love with fans. Impossible though to others it seems,
  I call you,* [Name,] *in my dreams.*

* Put four quartz crystals around the picture and candle, one in each
  corner and blow out the candle.

* Repeat for two more days, adding crystals.

* Leave the candle in the crystal square to burn through.

* Keep the quartz with the picture.

* Perhaps further your own career through reality TV and talent shows
  until you and the celebrity are in the same circles. Alternatively, you may
  meet a person with similar looks and fall in love.

If Your or Your Partner's Ex or Jealous Friends Are Stirring Up Trouble for You on Social Media

YOU WILL NEED

Pictures of those causing trouble on your screen while you're offline, placed in a horizontal row ⋆ Green crystals (preferably malachites) for each person sending you nastiness via social media, placed along the front of the computer ⋆ A purse or drawstring bag

TIMING

During the waning moon

THE SPELL

* Go along the row right to left, deleting the first picture and saying, *Now you are deleted, your power is gone and done. I shut you up, you are defeated, and so I have won.*

* Place the first crystal, right to left, in the bag, repeating the spell words.

* Continue deleting until you have an empty screen and all the crystals are in the bag.

* Put up a picture of you and your love on social media, and block the troublemakers.

If You Are So in Love You Can't Concentrate on Your Studies

A sprig of fresh rosemary ✳ A book you use for study

TIMING

When you can't concentrate

THE SPELL

✳ Hold the rosemary and say, *Rosemary for remembrance, I think of you night and day. But I must for now concentrate, and let love wait. My assignments won't go away.*

✳ Open the book at a page you need to study and say, *You're always with me, it drives me crazy, the facts are hazy. So for now I must keep you locked away, and when I'm finished, we can go out to play.*

✳ Place the rosemary in a page you have already studied.

✳ Replace the rosemary every time you study.

If You Aren't Sure Whether You Want a Girlfriend or a Boyfriend As Your Lasting Love

YOU WILL NEED

Red flower heads for a boy and an equal number of white flower heads for a girl ★ A basket or pouch to hold the flowers ★ A small purse or pouch

TIMING

By a fast-flowing river

THE SPELL:

* Cast red and white flowers alternately in the water, saying softly and continuously, *Reach out my heart. Reach out my soul. Send to me the love who will make me whole. The one who will inspire me, whose mind is with mine as one, that we may be together, till time itself is run.*

* Save one red and one white flower and keep the petals of those in a small bag or purse to carry with you until the petals fade.

If You Are Uncertain Which Is Your True Gender and You Are Being Pressured into Relationships That Do Not Feel Right

YOU WILL NEED

Your favorite fruits * A blender

TIMING

When you can be alone

THE SPELL

* Place the fruits in the blender and put your hands around the blender before switching it on. Say, *Mix and blend. Let other people's unwanted pressures end.*

* Switch on the machine and move your dominant hand clockwise on the right side of the blender and the other hand counterclockwise on the other side of the machine, not touching it, saying, *The right love at the right time, let me see. That I will know with certainty, whoever for me is meant to be.*

* Drink the smoothie, saying, *I will find the right love when I am sure, of my own true perfect identity. Until then, world, leave me be.*

If You Are Being Pressured to Have Sex Before You Are Ready

YOU WILL NEED

Romantic background music ✶ Strawberries
✶ A small electric fan ✶ Paper hearts cut
from pink paper, covering a table

TIMING

Before your love arrives

THE SPELL

* Put on some romantic music and eat a strawberry, saying, *Strawberries not beer, romancing, soft lights. Sweet music I would hear.*

* Eat a second strawberry and say, *Passion I know has its place, but our romance is not a race. Love me tenderly, be subtle, be sweet. I'm not a dinner for you to eat.*

* Put on the fan at low speed and let the paper hearts blow across the table, saying, *Feed me chocolates, bring me flowers. We've years to make love, not minutes or hours. I'm not ready so don't pressure me, for when we make love, right it must be.*

* Turn off the fan, scoop up the hearts, hiding them in corners of the room.

* Feed your love the strawberries.

If Your Lover Doesn't Want You to Go Away to College

YOU WILL NEED

A flower pot with soil ✳ Sunflower seeds
✳ Two matching rose quartz hearts or crystals

TIMING

The day before you leave

THE SPELL

✳ Outdoors set the pot of soil and around it make ever-widening seed circles on the ground, saying, *Parting is such sweet sorrow, for I will leave you on the morrow. I must go, my dreams pursue. But it's not the end for me and you.*

✳ Bury one of the rose quartz hearts or crystals in the soil.

✳ Bury some of the seeds as well, saying, *Loss and gain, there will be pain, but I would yearn for what I did not learn. And so by staying unwillingly, you would only have half of me.*

✳ Take the pot with you to college, give the other rose quartz heart or crystal to your love, and arrange to meet during a break.

If You Have Lost Your Confidence Because an Ex Has Told You That You Are Fat and Ugly or Useless in Bed

YOU WILL NEED

A mirror * A soft white cloth

TIMING

When sunlight reflects in the mirror

THE SPELL

* Gaze into the mirror, saying, *I look and see, what you say about me. Fat and ugly, useless in bed. Stop, no, what I see reflected in me, is only your malice and jealousy.*

* Polish the mirror with the cloth, going in counterclockwise circles and saying, *Beautiful/gorgeous I am, and beautiful/gorgeous shall I be, once I step right away, from your distorted vision of me.*

* Move away from the mirror with one last smile and go out into the sunshine.

If You Suddenly Fall in Love with Someone Who Has Always Been Your Best Friend

YOU WILL NEED

A photo of you when you were kids * A photo of
you together now * A box of individually wrapped
candies * A red ribbon * Rose petals or potpourri

TIMING

When you realize you are in love

THE SPELL

* Put the photos side by side.

* Enclose them in a circle of candies, saying, *Summer days, candy ways, you were always there. Climbing trees, what a tease, pulling at my hair.*

* Put the photos together, new one on top, and, using the ribbon, tie them together with three bows.

* Surround the candy circle with a heart shape of rose petals, saying, *My best friend, we will share, passion, joy and more. Take my hand and together, we'll walk forever through love's open door.*

* Keep the rose petals in a bowl until they fade.

* Share the candies.

If Your Parents Are Trying to Set You up with a Suitable Partner from Their Own Religion or Culture, but You Are in Love with Another

YOU WILL NEED

A box of used matches ∗ A small piece of paper ∗ A blue pen ∗ An empty matchbox

TIMING

Saturday, the day of breaking boundaries

THE SPELL

∗ Hold the box of used matches, saying, *Matchmaker, matchmaker, making a match, I do not seek. You may persist, every hour of the week, yet will I resist.*

∗ Throw away the box of used matches. On the paper write in small print with the blue pen the name of your true love and fold the paper. Place it in the empty matchbox, saying, *Matchmaker, matchmaker, this is his/her name. True love will overcome this cruel power game.*

∗ Hide the matchbox, and every day, open the box and say your true love's name.

If You and Your Love Want to Go Traveling, but Your Parents Object

A box of pins ✳ A map of where you want
to travel ✳ A magnet ✳ A cloth

TIMING

Before booking your tickets

THE SPELL

✳ Scatter the pins across the map, saying, *Please set me free. The world my love and I must see. I will return safe and sensible be, but right now this is our priority.*

✳ Draw the pins on the magnet, shutting them and the magnet in the box for the pins and say, *With guilt you try to keep me here, but I cannot be restricted by your fear.*

✳ Open the box and scatter the pins across the map again, leaving the magnet in the box, and say, *Give me your blessing to go freely, and I will come back willingly.*

✳ Gather the pins in a cloth, and tie it with the magnet inside. Take the map with you on your travels.

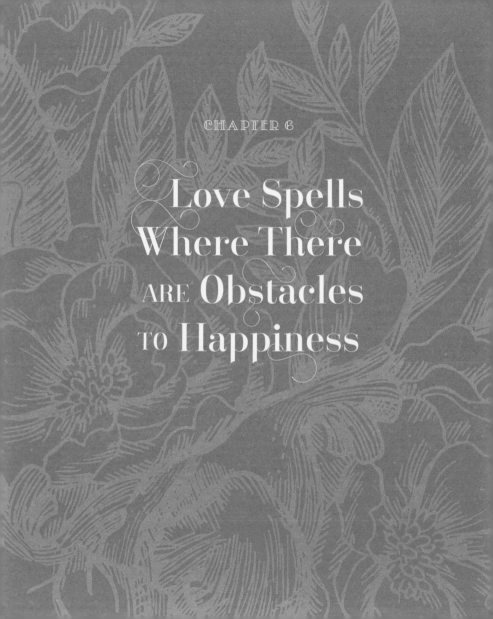

CHAPTER 6

Love Spells Where There ARE Obstacles TO Happiness

The path of true love never runs smooth, goes the old saying. But, given goodwill and honest intentions, many obstacles can be overcome. This chapter deals with those times when things go wrong or are clearly heading for disaster. Sometimes spells can steer love back on course, remove temptations, and keep us from unwise behavior. For almost every relationship reaches a crisis point at some time, and when a couple has been together for a while, a partner fearing aging and the loss of libido may act suddenly immaturely or irresponsibly in hopes of regaining lost youth. Also, interference from relatives or ex-partners, problems with children and stepchildren, and a demanding career that leaves no time for leisure can all drive a wedge between a couple.

As you read more of the book, you will see spells for similar issues coming from different angles, for the story of love is timeless and the same kinds of problems occur for people of different ages and situations. So, this chapter is an optimistic one, seeking solutions through magick to supplement earthly efforts and sometimes offering that magical impetus to overcome obstacles when all else has failed. If, in spite of everything, you can't go on, the chapter on love endings later in the book will help to ease the parting and help to move on to new life and even love.

A Plate-Smashing Spell If Your Partner Suddenly Says S/He No Longer Loves You and Wants a Divorce

YOU WILL NEED

An old plate * A photo of the two of you, cut in half * Glue * A new plate

TIMING

Monday

THE SPELL

* Smash the old plate safely, saying, *Smashed and ended, can't be mended. You say throw our love away.*

* Stick the halves of the photo together by gluing them onto a new plate, and say, *Not as good as new, but we are not yet through. I bind this situation, without hesitation. For your new life you must wait, for it's not too late. Our love is not a broken plate.*

* Put the new plate in a safe place. Touch it every day, saying, *Wait, love is not a broken plate. For us it is not too late. Wait for the instability to end.*

If Your Love Is Staying Out Late, Sending Secret Texts, and You Are Suspicious That S/he Is Having an Affair

YOU WILL NEED

An apple * A paring knife

TIMING

Wednesday morning

THE SPELL

* Bite into the apple and leave the remainder until it begins to turn brown.

* Hold the browning apple and say, *Eaten away, cannot be left. Cut off the bad, yet there is good still to be had.*

* Cut off the brown, eat the rest, and then say, *Not the end, too much laughter, too many tears. For a moment of madness, we can't destroy all these years.*

* Throw away the brown part, saying, *I banish this attack, restore the common sense you* [name your partner] *lack. For I will not surrender without a fight. Giving in won't make it right.*

* Bury the core and the seeds, saying, *Grow again, not without pain. But our lasting love shall not be in vain.*

* Repeat the spell weekly.

If Your Love Still Maintains Regular Overfriendly Contact with a Former Girlfriend or Boyfriend

YOU WILL NEED

The name of your partner and the friend, written in white on a white sheet of paper ✴ Nine hairs from your partner's hairbrush and nine of yours, bound together with White thread on a piece of thin red cord
✴ Tape

TIMING

During the waning moon

THE SPELL

✴ Fold the paper small and bind it with the red cord, making nine knots and saying, [name partner], *I bind, I wind, I find you mine. S/he must go, it shall be so. Your time together is over and done. S/he shall from your life henceforth be gone.*

✴ Tape the knotted paper to the underside of the doormat, or if you think it will be found there, bury it in a planter as near to the front door as possible.

If an Ex Keeps Your Partner Dangling Like a Puppet on a String

YOU WILL NEED

Paper, scissors, and glue to make two
finger puppets * String

TIMING

During the end of the waning moon cycle

THE SPELL

* Make two finger puppets, one to represent your partner and one his/her ex.

* Attach them to strings, and placing one on the index finger of each hand, make them dance, saying, *Puppet on a string. S/He can make you do anything. And so when s/he calls you always go, never able to say wait or no.*

* Cut your partner's strings and hang the ex's puppet on a bush or tree far away from your home.

* Hide your partner's puppet in a plant or bush in or near your home, saying, *Now you are free, not to dance at my command, but walking together, hand in hand.*

If Your Partner's Children Are Horrible to You and Coming between You and Your Partner

A chess set * A chessboard

Saturday

* Put two pawns, one in each color, for you and your partner, in the center of the chessboard.

* Put a knight for each boy and a castle piece for each girl in the same color as your partner's pawn, between you and your partner, saying, *Pawns in the game, the rules your children make. By winning this and every match, our relationship they'll break.*

* Replace your pawn with a king/queen and your partner's pawn with a king/queen in his/her color.

* Move the children's pieces and your pawns off the board, saying, *Checkmate, your power is through. When we're on the same side, and not torn in two, we totally and utterly outrank you.*

If Money Is Draining out Because of Your Partner's Constant Gambling

Three gambling chips or three plastic counters from any game * Salt in a plastic bowl with a lid

TIMING

During the waning moon

THE SPELL

* Bury the chips in the salt, saying, *You complain I nag, stop your fun. but you lose far more, than you ever won. It destroys our love, your gambling ways. I juggle finances every day.*

* Bury the sealed container in the earth for seven days, then dig it up, wash it out well, and fill it with water with the gambling chips in it.

* Put it in the freezer, saying, *Frozen shall be your gambling days. If you love me, mend your ways.*

* Leave it in the freezer indefinitely.

If Your Partner's Excessive Drinking or Drug Taking Is Destroying Your Relationship

A red candle in a candleholder
* A bowl of salt

TIMING

At the very end of the moon cycle

THE SPELL

* Light the candle and say, *You tell me that you care for me, but I can see you love your drinking/drugs far more. Unless you change, you'll soon be out the door.*

* Sprinkle salt in the flame, saying, *Burn away, turn away, fever of intensity, that destructive you will no longer be. For in the end, you must see. It's drinking/drugs or choose me.*

* Leave the candle to burn through, remove any remaining wax, and wash the candleholder well.

* Each week use progressively smaller red candles as you repeat the spell.

115

If Your In-Laws or Parents Are Constantly Interfering in Your Relationship

YOU WILL NEED

A red pen ✳ A piece of white paper
✳ A red penScissors ✳ A crystal

TIMING

Before a visit

THE SPELL

✳ In blue, draw the outline of two figures, hand in hand, in the center of the paper to represent you and your partner.

✳ In red, draw the outline of progressively larger figures that enclose your two figures, one red outline for each additional person who's interfering.

✳ Begin cutting away the outer figures, one by one, saying, *I cut your interference right away, your positive presence may willingly stay. You have your own lives, we have ours. For your unasked-for intrusion, happiness sours.*

✳ Keep cutting until the two inner figures are free.

✳ Put the paper scraps under a large stone outside. Decorate your figures and hang them on a crystal at a window.

If Your Partner's Job or Business Always Takes Priority and You Feel You Might As Well Be Single

YOU WILL NEED

Two pieces of paper, one with your name and the other with his/hers, each enclosed in a circle, drawn in pencil * A small box * Red string * An eraser

TIMING

Friday

THE SPELL

* Put his/her paper in the box, tie the box with red string, and stand it on top of your paper so your name is covered.

* Say, *I might as well be single, though your pockets/purse with profits jingles. I spend my life at home alone, polishing your empty throne.*

* Lift the box off your name and cut the string, saying, *From your box I set you free, willingly or not. Explore life with me.*

* Erase both circles and cut out the names, putting the names tied together with red string down the back of your partner's favorite chair.

If You Are Always Arguing about How to Bring Up the Children

YOU WILL NEED

Two lilac incense sticks in separate holders, one on either end of the table * An empty double incense holder in the center of the table * A bowl of sand or soil

TIMING

Friday

THE SPELL

* Light each incense stick, one for you and one for your partner.

* Move the incense sticks closer and closer together. When they reach the center, transfer the smoking incense sticks to the double holder, saying, *Moving closer, to middle ground. Given love between us, solutions can be found.*

* Cross the incense sticks so the smoke mingles, saying, *Let's agree to disagree, compromise as best can be. For when the kids are grown and flown, it will be you and me alone.*

* Plunge both sticks, lighted end down, into the soil, saying, *The end of quarreling, unity bring. None shall divide us, not even our offspring.*

If Your Partner Is Obsessed with Do-It-Yourself Projects and You Are Tired of Living in a Construction Site

YOU WILL NEED

A hammer ✳ Four nails ✳ A piece of wood
(there's plenty around, no doubt)
✳ Paint

TIMING

During the crescent moon

THE SPELL

✳ Hammer in the first nail on the wood vigorously, saying, *Hammer, bang, crash, clatter, crunch and smash. My home is just a building site. I fear it will continue until I'm old, not right.*

✳ Hammer in the second nail more softly, saying, *Home sweet home, let's clean up the mess. Enjoy time together, quit all this stress.*

✳ Hammer in the third nail slowly, saying, *Noise and disruption now you will cease. My home sweet home shall be a place of peace.*

✳ Throw away the fourth nail.

✳ Paint HOME SWEET HOME on the wood and display it.

If You Want Exotic Vacations and Your Partner Won't Go Farther Than the End of the Street

YOU WILL NEED

A pile of vacation brochures * Nine metal tacks * A small bag or purse

TIMING

Before your partner comes home

THE SPELL

* Put the brochures on his/her favorite chair with the tacks on top of the brochures, sharp end facing upward.

* Pass both hands clockwise over the tacks a few inches above them, saying, *Move your butt, let's get life moving. For our life needs improving.*

* Scoop up all the tacks and put them in the bag, saying, *A short sharp shock is what you need, and I'll give you one indeed. Quit your armchair fair and square—or you'll find I'll not be there.*

* Leave the brochures on the chair and offer him/her a choice of venues. Keep the bag of tacks in the same room in a safe place.

If Your Partner's Best Friend Is Always Hanging Around and Insists on Being Included in Everything

YOU WILL NEED

A printout of a picture of the three of you together
* Scissors

TIMING

When you are expecting a visit

THE SPELL

* Hold the picture, saying, *Two's company, three's a crowd. To leave us alone is allowed.*

* Carefully cut out as much as you can of the friend from the photo. Put that over the doorframe of the front door or taped under the doormat, saying, *Stay away, you waif and stray. You're no longer permitted to enter here, except by invite. Is that clear?*

* Have a new picture taken of just you and your partner to display.

If Your Partner Is Helping a Colleague or Neighbor through an Emotional Crisis and You Suspect That Is Just an Excuse for Them to Get Together

YOU WILL NEED

A mug and a spoon ⋆ A green tea bag or
loose green tea ⋆ Sugar

TIMING

When you know they are having a heart-to-heart

THE SPELL

* Make a cup of green tea and stir it counterclockwise nine times, adding heaps of sugar and saying, *Tea and sympathy arouses in me, suspicion s/he offers my partner more, a flattered ego and an open door.*

* Pour out the tea under cold running water, saying, *Pouring cold water on this cozy encounter. If you're sincere, why not ask your mom or counselor? My partner's sympathies belong to me. Get someone else to make your tea.*

* When your partner comes home, offer to make him/her a cup of tea.

If There Are Major Quarrels in Your or Your Partner's Family and You Are Stuck in the Middle

A long red cord, knotted once in the middle for you
and your partner united, and, near both ends,
knotted to represent each of the warring factions
* Scissors * Artificial flowers, ribbons, bells, and crystals

TIMING

When this is causing trouble between you and your partner

THE SPELL

* Hold the cord tightly at both ends and say, *Tug-of-war, for our emotions, shouting, sniping, causing commotion. I am not a referee, please don't stir up trouble between my partner and me.*

* Cut the knots off each of the ends and discard them, saying, *No more will we be tangled in your strife. We will step back and focus on our life.*

* Decorate the remaining cord containing the joint knot with tiny artificial flowers, ribbons, bells, and crystals, and hang it in a front-facing window.

If You and Your Ex-Partner Still Share a House and S/He Won't Move Out for Financial Reasons

YOU WILL NEED

Five hairs from your ex-partner's hairbrush or comb
∗ Yellow thread ∗ A thin yellow cord
∗ A small item your partner once gave you

TIMING

During the waning moon

THE SPELL

∗ Tie the hairs with thread to the cord and the cord around the item, saying, *I detach from you. We both know this relationship is through. I need my space, my privacy, and so I bind you from holding on to me.*

∗ Starting from any shared area, each day conceal the item closer and closer to the front door, repeating the spell words.

∗ Once outdoors, untie the item, dispose of the chord, and take the item to a thrift shop, saying, *Unwanted goods, should have gone long ago. Now removed permanently, like your presence shall be from me.*

If One of You Is Very Tidy and One of You Is a Clutterer at Home

YOU WILL NEED

A web of tangled green thread
* An unopened spool of green thread
* A green bag * Fresh rosemary
sprigs * A raffia or copper hoop
* Small red baubles or solar lights

TIMING

Thursday

THE SPELL

* Put the web of tangled green threads and the spool of green thread in the bag and shake it well ten times, saying ten times, *Mix us together, tie up the ends. Separate is a nightmare, but with love we can blend.*

* Take out the spool of thread and cut off lengths of thread, also trimming the web of threads so some cut-off threads are straight, using both alternately to secure the rosemary to the hoop, saying, *Order and chaos blended as one. Rosemary brings compromise under the sun.*

* Decorate the hoop with small red baubles or solar lights. Hang it outside the front door and refresh it regularly, repeating the spell words.

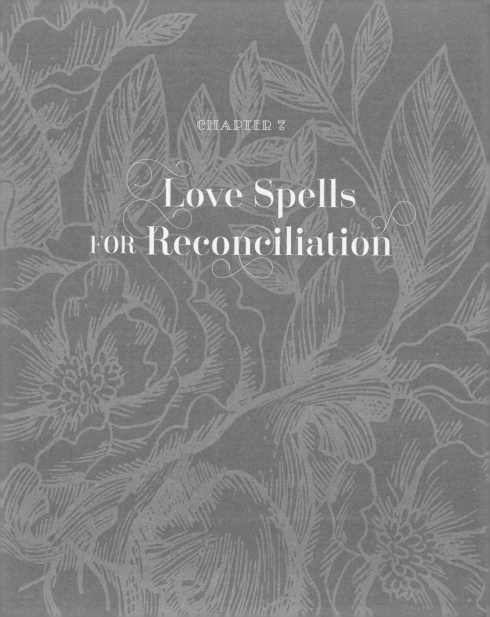

CHAPTER 7

Love Spells
FOR Reconciliation

There are many reasons for a relationship to come to an end, but oftentimes splits are caused by unresolved issues from the past, before you met, or even past lives; ex-partners or parents who still interfere; irresponsible friends; children from previous relationships making trouble; or a fear of commitment because of previous hurts. When a couple live together for the first time, differences in lifestyle and priorities may arise that were not apparent before. One or both partners may change, or hit a midlife crisis and seek excitement with a new partner, hoping to alleviate his/her inner turmoil stemming from aging or lack of success.

Sometimes a relationship can't be mended, especially where there has been deep betrayal or one partner is set on walking and staying away. But given goodwill on both sides, and a little magick, a new and stronger relationship can be forged that will last a lifetime because it was tested and survived.

Reconciliation spells are excellent not only for banishing sorrows and resentment from the breakup and doubts that may creep in, but also for clearing the influence of those who stand in the way of togetherness. These spells can wipe the slate clean and give the reconciliation a good chance of working.

The spells in this chapter are effective whether you have split from someone you deeply care for but have only known for a relatively short time or a partner of many years.

An All-Purpose Reconciliation Spell

Two almost-burned-through green candles
* Two new green candles

TIMING

During the waxing moon

THE SPELL

* Light the almost-burned-through candles, saying, *All the harsh words that have been spoken, all the vows that have been broken, yet love's flame still dimly burns, not too late to let love return.*

* Light each new candle from one old candle, saying, *Love can again burn bright. The bad dark times turn to light.*

* Leave the old candles to burn through.

* Blow softly into each new candle flame, saying, *Burn bright, and light the way to happiness.*

* After a few minutes, blow out the new candles and each evening relight them for a short time. When they are almost burned, replace them, and, if you wish, repeat the spell.

If You Wish to Get Back with Your Ex-Partner But S/He Has Moved On

YOU WILL NEED

A green candle ★ Two green cords of the same length
★ An old photo of the two of you ★ Red thread

TIMING

During the crescent moon

THE SPELL

* Light the candle and singe one end of each cord with the candle flame, saying, *What was between us may seem gone, but in my heart, love lives on.*

* When the ends are cool, tie them together in a double knot, saying, *I seek our love to grow again, I ask this dream is not in vain.*

* Complete a circle by joining the other ends of the cords with another double knot, saying, *I would not steal you from your new love, nor wish him/her ill. But should that relationship unhappy prove, the circle of togetherness is waiting still.*

* Attach an old photo of the two of you with the red thread to the circle of cords, but go on with your life.

If the Person Who Caused the Split Is Still in Your Lives

YOU WILL NEED

Four clay figures or small dolls ✳ Red ribbon ✳ A small
basket filled with greenery ✳ A piece of silk

TIMING

During the waning moon

THE SPELL

✳ Tie two of the figures, to represent you and your partner, face-to-face,
   with the ribbon, saying, *We two start anew. What's done is done,
   the past is through.*

✳ Put the other two figures in the basket, representing the other person
   and his/her new love to be (or maybe one already found), saying,
   *I bear no ill will, to s/he who drove us apart. But from our lives, s/he must
   now depart.*

✳ Float their figures on water, saying, *Look no more on my love with envy.
   Flow away, go away, and new love see.*

✳ Wrap your two figures in silk.

If Children or Family Are Pressuring You to Reconcile with Your Ex-Partner

A trailing plant for you and one for your ex-partner ∗ Smaller trailing plants, one for each of the people pressuring you.

TIMING

Wednesday

THE SPELL

* Tie a frond from your plant to your ex-partner's and to each of the other plants, saying, *You want the best for me I know, but my own way I must go. Not what you think I should do and be, from your expectations set me free.*

* Cut the connections between your plant and your ex's and the other plants.

* Plant the family greenery away from yours and your ex's.

* Leave your ex-partner's plant close to yours, but not touching, saying, *If it is right we shall reconciled be, but the link must grow naturally. Together reaching for the sun, or knowing that love's course is run.*

If You're Not Sure You Can Forgive and Forget

YOU WILL NEED

A broken but beautiful necklace * An empty
bowl * A new string * A jewelry clasp

TIMING

Monday at sunset

THE SPELL

* Pull off all the beads or crystals from the necklace one by one, dropping them into the bowl, naming for each a hurt or injustice. When you have finished, say, *Trust that was broken, cruel words spoken. Can't be mended, yet love is not ended.*

* Thread the beads, one by one, onto the new string, naming, for each bead, good qualities in your ex-partner and dreams you would still like to fulfil together.

* Then say, *We must make our relationship anew, walk away from the past. For only by leaving what is broken behind, can we make a love that will last.*

* Tie the ends together and get a new clasp to secure it. Wear the necklace or give it to your partner.

To Wipe the Slate Clean and Really Start Again

A child's blackboard or a piece of slate
* Red chalk * White chalk

TIMING

A rainy day

THE SPELL

* Write on the board in red chalk, BITTER AND ANGRY AM I, THAT YOU SHOULD HURT ME AND MAKE ME CRY. YET I WANT TO STAY, EVEN THOUGH OTHERS SAY I SHOULD GO AWAY.

* Leave the board in the rain or pour water over it if it is dry weather, saying, *Wipe the slate clean.*

* In white chalk, write, WE CAN START AGAIN, LEAVE BEHIND THE PAIN. REGAIN TRUST, IN YOU I MUST. I HAVE WIPED THE SLATE CLEAN.

If the Issues That Split You up Haven't Been Fully Resolved and Are Spoiling the Reconciliation

YOU WILL NEED

A piece of white paper with jagged black lines drawn all over it

TIMING

At the end of the moon cycle

THE SPELL

* Hold the paper, saying, *Papering over the cracks, just won't work. For old troubles lurk, waiting to come back.*

* Crush the paper into a ball, then throw it higher and higher, saying, as a chant, faster and faster, *Need to start a whole new ball game, let it all come tumbling out, scream and shout. Clear the air, fair and square, and then begin again.*

* When you can chant and throw the wadded-up paper ball no higher, toss the paper ball as far away as possible.

* On a blank sheet of paper, list the thorny issues you and your partner need to tackle honestly and openly to really start again.

If Family Members Took Sides When You Split and Now Oppose a Reconciliation

YOU WILL NEED

A dark stone for each person opposing the reconciliation ★ Two clear quartz crystals, representing you and your ex-partner ★ A bowl of water in which you have dissolved black ink ★ A spoon ★ Flower heads

TIMING

Monday

THE SPELL

* Pile the dark stones on top of your and your ex's quartz crystals.

* Stir the water with a spoon, saying, *Muddying the waters, with who's wrong and who's right. Burying us, beneath their insistence, it's simply black or white.*

* One by one drop the dark stones into the inky water, saying, *Arguments, musts, and oughts, just confuse our loving thoughts. Whatever they choose to say, together shall we forever stay.*

* Pour cold water from a running tap into the bowl until the water in the bowl is clear.

* Put the dark stones outside.

* Set your crystals with flower heads into the clean water.

If You Plan to Move and Make a New Start

YOU WILL NEED

A mint or hyssop infusion made from a tea bag in a mug
of boiling water, strained ∗ A few small items from
the home you're leaving that represent sad memories
∗ A small cedar smudge stick or a coil of sweetgrass
∗ Small new items, bought together for your new home

TIMING

The week before you move

THE SPELL

∗ Sprinkle drops of the infusion in nine counterclockwise circles around
the items that conjure up sad memories, saying softly, *The old sorrow,
the past sadness, I now do cleanse, leaving only gladness.*

∗ Pass the lighted smudge stick around the new items nine times clockwise
or burn a sweetgrass coil next to them, saying, *Here is our lovely fresh
start. I greet our new life with a happy heart.*

∗ Give the old cleansed items to a charity shop. Make the new items
among the first things taken into your new home.

For a Make or Break Vacation

Red, yellow, green, and blue ribbons,
as many as you wish ✳ Houseplants

TIMING

A few days before the vacation

THE SPELL

✳ Tie the ribbons to the plants at home, touching the different colors
 and saying, *Red for passion, yellow for joy, green for love, blue for fidelity—
 these are the hopes I will carry with me.*

✳ The day before the vacation, untie and pack the ribbons in
 your luggage.

✳ Once at the resort, tie the ribbons to an outdoor tree, repeating the
 spell words and adding, *Make not break, happiness assuredly waits.*

If You Want to Stay Together, But the Joy and Spontaneity Aren't There Anymore

YOU WILL NEED

Rose or sandalwood fragrance
* Rose or sandalwood bath essence (if you're alone)

TIMING

A rainy day

THE SPELL

* Anoint with fragrance the center of your hairline, your brow,
  the base of your throat, and your inner wrist points for your heart,
  saying, *Fill me once again with passion, joy outpouring, and love restoring.*
  Feelings flood through me like the falling rain.

* Stand in the rain without a coat, repeating the spell words
  until you are soaked.

* Have a bath or shower with your partner, or make love in the rain.
  If you're alone, anoint yourself with rose or sandalwood bath essence
  as you shower, repeating the spell words.

Healing Bad Memories If You Stay in the Same Place after the Reconciliation

YOU WILL NEED

A large bowl of lavender, musk, or sandalwood potpourri
★ Four empty smaller bowls ★ Sandalwood or musk oil

TIMING

During the crescent moon

THE SPELL

* Place the large bowl of lavender, musk, or sandalwood potpourri in the room where you argued most. Mix the potpourri with your hands or a spoon, saying progressively more softly and slowly, *heal the silences, the angry words, absorb resentment lingering. Remove everything, except the love and care, for that always will be there.*

* When the words fade, put some potpourri in each bowl, adding a drop or two of oil to all five bowls, saying, *Let all sorrow and reproaches cease, leave only peace.*

* Set the smaller bowls around your home.

* Add a drop of oil weekly to all five bowls, repeating both sets of spell words.

* Keep the potpourri until the fragrance fades.

If Your Ex-Partner Wants Reconciliation for All the Wrong Reasons

YOU WILL NEED

A wooden or metal bowl (partly filled with coins) ✳ A photo of your ex with you/your family smiling, to create the right impression

TIMING

Wednesday

THE SPELL

✳ Shake the bowl continuously, saying, *All the wrong reasons, eager the world to impress, playing happy families, not a sign of stress. Money, security are what you prize, being the good partner/family man in the world's eyes.*

✳ Shake the bowl faster, chanting faster, and end by banging the bowl down on a surface, saying, *From here you're banned, falsehood in you I simply can't stand. Enough of playing happy families. You don't want me, only security.*

✳ Take out the door key and send the photo, mixed with other possessions you are sending on to his/her new address, as a reminder of what s/he has lost.

If You Are Torn between Two Lovers and Both Are Demanding That You Choose Which One You Want

Both lovers' pictures on the same computer screen ✦ A selfie on a second screen

TIMING

Anytime you feel the need

THE SPELL

* Point to the picture of the longer-lasting relationship, saying, *Security, stability you offer to me. Why can't I accept what's in front of me?*

* Point to the other picture, saying, *My heart races, my pulse chases, passion, excitement, ecstasy, but mixed with a dose of uncertainty.*

* Place your selfie over both the images so they are obscured, saying, *Until I know who is really me, between you both torn I shall be.*

* Remove their images from the screen and print your image large, saying, *Me, only me, give me space to see, which of you is right for me, or to start alone separately. Until I choose don't pressure me.*

* Go away alone and hang the picture of yourself in a prominent position on the wall.

If You Are in a New Relationship, but Can't Stop Thinking About Your Ex-Partner

YOU WILL NEED:

A smoky quartz or apache tear crystal, that is dark but slightly transparent

TIMING

The end of the moon cycle

THE SPELL

* Hold the crystal in your open, cupped hands, saying, *The past is gone, and old love over and done. So why do I dream constantly of you* [Name], *when we both have moved on, and know it is through?*

* Close your hands around the crystal and whisper into it all the feelings you still have for your ex-partner.

* Find a quiet, beautiful place, and bury your crystal somewhere where you went together, saying, *Not in this lifetime, was it meant to be. I let you go reluctantly. Reconciled to the new lives we chose, and so this chapter do I close.*

A Reconciliation Ritual to Be Carried Out Alone or with a Partner

Note: If you are both doing the spell, do alternate actions and speak alternate words.

YOU WILL NEED

Dying leaves in a bowl ✳ Edible seeds in another bowl ✳ An evergreen tree

TIMING

During the crescent moon

THE SPELL

✳ Sit on the ground, taking a leaf and naming a regret or sorrow about what went wrong.

✳ Let it blow away.

✳ Continue until you have named everything or the leaves are gone.

✳ Take a seed, naming a joint dream or hope for your future together.

✳ Leave the rest of the seeds in the bowl.

✳ Plant your evergreen, saying, *We shall not mourn the passing of what can be no more. Our love shall grow stronger than before. Evergreen shall it be throughout the years, no more dead leaves and no more tears.*

✳ Plant the remaining seeds around the tree.

A Candle Reconciliation Ritual
Alone or with Both of You

*Note: Again, you can divide and adapt the words
and actions if you are both taking part.*

YOU WILL NEED

Two separate green candles set between a larger green one

TIMING

The first day of the week or month

THE SPELL

* Light the candle at left for yourself, saying, *As we grew apart, the flame between us flickered and went out. But now we rekindle the light anew, free from sorrow and from doubt, always to burn between me and you.*

* Light the candle at right, repeating the spell words.

* Holding a lighted candle in each hand, say, *Our love together shall forever burn bright. None can come between us or dim that light.*

* Leave all the candles to burn through as a reminder that you don't need to lose yourself to be in love.

If Your Ex-Partner Is Too Stubborn to Come Home

YOU WILL NEED

A white candle in a heatproof glass holder

TIMING

After dark on a night with no wind

THE SPELL

* Light the candle and set it in an uncurtained window facing the front of the house.

* Blow softly into the flame and say, *Return to my arms, my life, and my heart, without recrimination or hesitation, blame or reproach, as though we have never been apart.*

* Carry the candle outside the front door, sheltering the flame and repeating the spell words. If the flame goes out, relight it.

* Go onto the lawn or into the street, saying the same spell words.

* Blow out the candle, saying, *follow the light. Come home to me, waiting for you this night.*

* Relight the candle in the window until you go to bed and make contact.

A Flowing Water Reconciliation Ritual
If Your Ex-Lover Won't Respond to Contact

YOU WILL NEED:

A clear glass bottle with a lid ★ Two gold
earrings or two gold-colored coins

TIMING

Early Sunday morning

THE SPELL

* Go to a flowing river, stream, or the ocean, where there are shallows.

* Scoop up water in the bottle and put on the lid, saying, *Flowing waters of the sea, send back I ask my love to me.*

* Throw into the river, stream, or ocean one piece of gold as an offering.

* Return at or near sunset and pour the water back, saying, *Flowing waters of the sea, I return what is yours. Send my love back to me.*

* Drop into the water the second tribute, turn, and do not look back.

* Make contact in a way you know will be received.

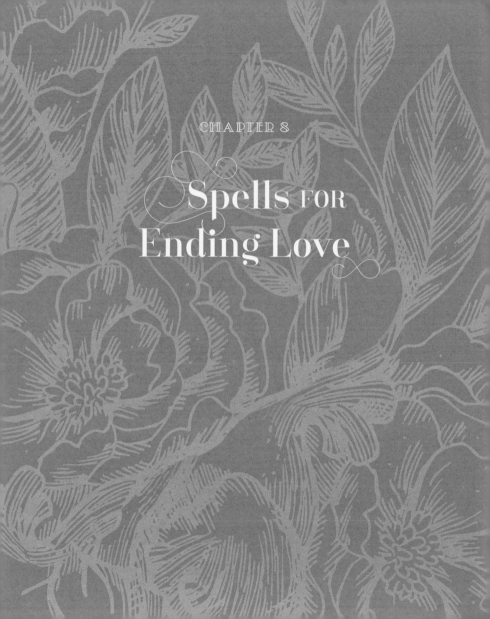

CHAPTER 8

Spells FOR Ending Love

ometimes love can't be mended, or only at the price of your health and well-being. But walking away, especially if there are children involved or you are financially tied to property or a business you share, may not be easy. If a relationship is abusive or controlling, you may lose your confidence and self-esteem and believe quite wrongly, but understandably, that the problems are your fault. There is increasing help for both men and women to escape abusive relationships, but spells can help to give you the strength to walk away when emotions have become clouded.

But for many relationships, long or short, it may be that the couple have grown apart, one has changed and wants new experiences and the other has not, or one is attracted to someone new. Parting is never easy and if there are children, beloved animals, and joint assets, the one partner may use these as a weapon. In such cases, it can take a lot of courage to persist, especially if your confidence has been eroded and your partner knows how to emotionally manipulate you.

Though some of the spells in this chapter can be adapted to be used by both parties to ease the pain of parting, many are a way of taking back your strength and power to give you the courage to walk away or ask your partner to leave.

If Your Partner Is a Constant Drama King/ Queen and You Want a Peaceful Life

YOU WILL NEED

A mask of a wicked king or queen from a toy shop
* Your cell phone

TIMING

After s/he has stormed out yet again

THE SPELL

* Hold the mask between your hands, saying, *Act 1, Scene 1, No idea what I said or did wrong. But you storm and rage, Posture and gesture and leave the stage, With an overloud song. I'm supposed to run after you, Make it all right. And we'll kiss and make up, Till the very next night.*

* Put down the mask, set your cell phone to silent for five minutes, find his/her picture on the phone, and dim the brightness. Say, Find another to give you applause. I leave the theater, Center stage is yours.

* Remove the image from your phone, put the mask in your recycling bin, and move on to a more harmonious love.

If Your Partner Is a Constant Drama King/ Queen and You Want a Peaceful Life

152

YOU WILL NEED

A mask of a wicked king or queen from a toy shop
* Your cell phone

TIMING

After s/he has stormed out yet again

THE SPELL

* Hold the mask between your hands, saying, *Act 1, Scene 1, no idea what I said or did wrong. But you storm and rage, posture and gesture and leave the stage, with an overloud song. I'm supposed to run after you, make it all right. And we'll kiss and make up, till the very next night.*

* Put down the mask, set your cell phone to silent for five minutes, find his/her picture on the phone, and dim the brightness. Say, *Find another to give you applause. I leave the theater, center stage is yours.*

* Remove the image from your phone, put the mask in your recycling bin, and move on to a more harmonious love.

If Your Partner Is Abusive and Makes You Feel It Is All Your Fault

YOU WILL NEED

A rag doll

TIMING

At the end of the moon cycle

THE SPELL

* Shake the doll hard, saying loudly, *All my fault you say, deserve all I get, afraid to go or to stay.*

* Shake the doll more gently, speaking in softer and slower tones, saying, *Yet I know I must go, make a new life of peace, for this abuse will never cease.*

* Hold the doll still in your arms and whisper, *The days of fear and helplessness are through. I will escape and so will you.*

* Hold your doll every day, repeating, *The days of fear and helplessness are through. I will escape and so will you.*

* When you leave, give the doll pride of place in your new home.

A Sand-Parting Rite for Setting Yourself Free from a Relationship Going Nowhere

YOU WILL NEED

A large spoon or small trowel ✳ A bowl of
sand ✳ Two separate containers, one with a lid

TIMING

At the end of the moon cycle

THE SPELL

* With a large spoon, begin putting the sand into separate containers, scooping alternately into each. Say softly and continuously, *Once we flowed together like grains of sand, once we walked through life hand in hand. Now with the blowing winds of time we separate, knowing that for reconciliation it is too late.*

* When you have divided the sand evenly, scatter your partner's sand outdoors, saying, *Go free, to where you will happy be, without me.*

* Put the lid on your container of sand and keep it until you settle with the right person who will join yours with new sand.

If Your Ex-Partner Is Holding the Children or Property over Your Head and So Making the Ending Harder Than It Need Be

YOU WILL NEED

A blue candle ✷ A thin red cord or strong string ✷ A pot of soil

TIMING

Saturday after dark

THE SPELL

✷ Light the candle. Tie a knot in the center of the cord, saying, *The cord between us once was long, the love between us then was strong. But now it is decaying, fraying, choking me. Let me go and set me free.*

✷ Hold the ends of the cord over the flame in both hands, so the knot is taut in the flame. As the knot breaks, repeat the spell words.

✷ Drop the burning cord into the soil and extinguish the candle. Bury the cord in the soil in the garden or in a planter, saying, *Let these power games rest in peace, so hostilities between us finally cease.*

To Rid Yourself of a Persistent Unwanted Admirer or Stalker

YOU WILL NEED

A dark purple candle, a gray candle, and a white candle in a row

TIMING

During the last three nights of the moon cycle

THE SPELL

* On night 1, light the dark purple candle, saying, *Our paths no longer shall entwine. You have your life, I have mine.*

* Extinguish the candle, if you're casting the spell to discourage a stalker's unwanted attentions, and add, *Be gone from my sphere, excluded from coming near.*

* On night 2, light the gray candle, saying, *Lost in the mists of obscurity, You no longer notice me.* If you're casting the spell to discourage a stalker's unwanted attentions, add the stalking prohibition.

* On night 3, light the white candle, saying, *I send your light, to s/he who will make you happy. No longer think of me.*

* If you're casting the spell to discourage a stalker's unwanted attentions, substitute, *This light so bright, hides me from your sight, excluded from ever coming near.*

* Leave the white candle to burn through. Dispose of the others.

To End a Relationship That You Have Outgrown When Everyone, Including Your Partner, Insists That You Are the Perfect Couple

YOU WILL NEED

Two pine or cedar incense sticks in separate holders ∗ Dried vervain or lemongrass (use herbs from split tea bags, if necessary) ∗ A bowl of soil or sand ∗ Two seedlings of your chosen herb

TIMING

During the new moon

THE SPELL

∗ Light the incense and scatter the herbs around the separate incense holders, counterclockwise, saying, *What you all see, as love is illusion, what we once had, is gone and done. I need to be free and move on.*

∗ Extinguish the incense sticks, lighted end down, in the soil, saying, *Love grown cold, shall not grow old. I sadly must disillusion, your delusion from reality.* [Name], *I need to grow separately.*

∗ Plant the seedlings, mixed with cooled ash in different places.

To Ease the Pain When Your Love Suddenly Leaves You Forever

A diffuser ✳ Lemon balm (melissa) or lemon verbena
fragrance oil ✳ An old piece of jewelry or an item s/he bought
you ✳ A new ring or piece of jewelry you have bought yourself

TIMING

Any evening

THE SPELL

* Light the diffuser candle to warm the water in the diffuser, saying,
  *Be as balm to my troubled soul, heal my sorrowing heart. When you walked
  out, never to return, you ripped my life apart.*

* Add lemon balm or verbena oil to the warmed water, saying,
  *Oil on troubled water, I shall live anew. Laugh again, and love once
  more, and so myself renew.*

* Take off the old jewelry, passing the new item through the
  fragrant smoke.

* When you feel ready, explore online some new activity or place.

* Put the old item away and wear the new one.

For Breaking Free from a Destructive Relationship When What Keeps You Is Fear of Being Alone

YOU WILL NEED

A computer (if you are not technologically savvy, you can draw on several sheets of paper)

TIMING

When you realize you want to be free

THE SPELL

* Draw on the screen (or on two sheets of paper) an outline of two featureless figures, not touching, but next to each other, saying, *Figures without features, all feelings gone. No connection between us, except my fear of being alone.*

* Draw two separate circles, one enclosing each figure, and say, *But I am alone anyway, you hurt and destroy me a little more each day.*

* Move each circle farther apart until both disappear off the screen and the screen is empty, saying, *Gone is the fear that keeps me here, I reclaim myself, face the pain, find my features again.*

* Put a smiling selfie of yourself in the middle of the screen and make it a screensaver or a profile picture.

For Letting Go of a Lover Who Keeps Coming Back, but Never Stays Faithful

YOU WILL NEED

A piece of black paper ★ A white crayon
A bucket of cold water ★ Tea tree or eucalyptus oil

TIMING

On the last day of the waning moon

THE SPELL

* On the paper draw in white crayon a figure walking away. Say as you hold it, *You walk away and then come back, promising it will all have changed. But within days it is just the same. This time you must stay away, your inconstant games I no longer play.*

* Drop the paper in the bucket, saying, *My love you have finally drowned in lies, I see only deceit in your eyes. And so love dies.*

* When the paper has disintegrated, drain off any water, dispose of the paper, and wash out the bucket in hot water with tea tree or eucalyptus oil.

For Finally Leaving a Love You Know Will Never Openly Be Yours

YOU WILL NEED

Twelve dark-colored stones, one for each month
★ Soil or sand ★ Birdseed

TIMING

At the beginning of a new month

THE SPELL

* Go to a quiet place, where you used to meet, where there is earth, sand, or grass.

* Using the stones, spell out the initials of your first names side by side, saying, *Through months and years, we have talked of the future we will share. But all that is left is futile tears. You can never openly for me be there.*

* Cover the initials over with soil, or sand, or dig them into the grass, scattering seeds on the surface to be eaten by birds, and say, *Our love in this lifetime can never be, and so at last I set us free.*

A Candle Parting for an Official Separation or Divorce, If You Still Need to See Your Ex Because of Children or Business Connections

YOU WILL NEED

A large white candle with two wicks ∗ Two smaller white candles, set on either side of the large candle ∗ A small square white candle, set in front of the large one to represent children or a joint business venture

TIMING

On the day the official papers are sent/received by you

THE SPELL

∗ Light the double-wick candle, saying, *Once we were in love, and we were one. Though those days now are gone, let peace and harmony between us come.*

∗ From each wick on the double-wick candle, light a single small candle, and then from each single candle the square candle, saying, *When we must meet, let it be as friends. With the dimming of this light, all bitterness ends.*

∗ Extinguish the double-wick candle and let the three separate candles burn through.

If the Separation Is Informal, But You Need to Get Closure to Move On

YOU WILL NEED

A purple cord long enough to tie around both of your own wrists loosely and leave a loop ★ Flowers

TIMING

Before sunset

THE SPELL

* Gently loop the cord around both your wrists, saying, *Hand part, you once precious to my heart. Love breaks, my heart aches. And yet I must move to my new start.*

* Pull the cord free, saying, *No more hand fast, love did not last. I loved you so, but now I let you go.*

* Holding the cord loosely in one hand, turn it three times counterclockwise, saying, *I unwind, I unbind, I find I am free. Regretfully, but it must be, unwound, unbound, my separate self once more is found.*

* Decorate the cord with flowers and hang it from a tree or bush.

After a Painful Parting or Divorce, When You Don't Want to Go On

YOU WILL NEED

A small kite

TIMING

At sunrise

THE SPELL

* Holding the kite in your nondominant hand, trace on the surface of the kite as you slowly say the words, *How can I go on without you? You won't even speak to me. If you don't want me, let go of my heart and set me free.*

* Find an open windy space, get your kite flying, and release it, saying, *I let you go, I release any hold on you. This love is through. Winds of the east, south, west, and north, carry my new life forth. Over land and over sea, where waits a new destiny.*

* Walk away and don't look back.

* Book a vacation as soon as practical.

If You Have to See the Person You Love with Someone Else Every Day

YOU WILL NEED

A semitransparent smoky quartz or apache tear crystal * A surreptitiously taken small picture of your old love and his/her new partner * Two musk incense sticks in separate holders, one set on either side of the picture

TIMING

At sunset

THE SPELL

* Put the crystal on top of the picture so it obscures their faces.

* Light the musk incense sticks and, holding one in each hand, spiral them counterclockwise around the outside of the picture, saying, *Let* [Names] *be cloaked in invisibility. That though them I must daily see, they will unnoticed and unnoticeable be.*

* When the incense is burned, remove the crystal.

* Scatter the ash on the picture.

* Seal it all in an envelope that you drop in the garbage.

* When you know you will meet them, hold the crystal and repeat the spell words.

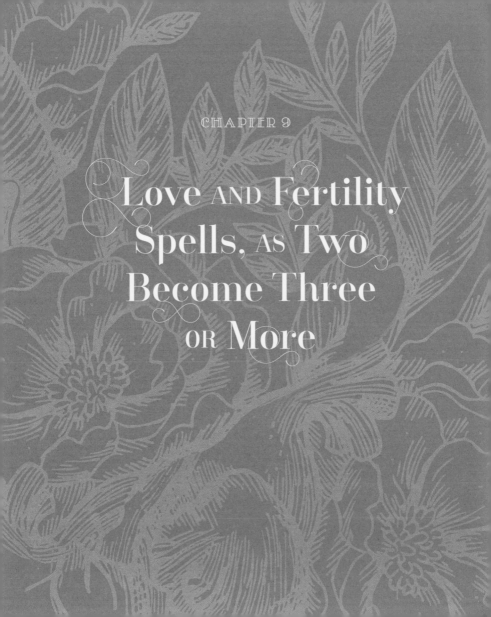

CHAPTER 9

Love AND Fertility Spells, AS Two Become Three OR More

In the modern world, couples who tend to have children later in life may panic if conception is slow to occur. And sometimes, though a first baby may be conceived quickly, subsequent infants may take longer to appear, probably because we are far busier and lovemaking with an existing child to care may need to be planned like a military operation. And let's not forget that same-sex couples and transgender men and women are often eager to have children of their own.

In my experience, fertility spells dramatically reduce anxiety and bring about or restore spontaneity to lovemaking, which overcomes many psychological and psychic barriers to conception. Indeed, even where there are physiological causes and IVF or artificial insemination are part of the process, the spells seem to help the body to relax at a very stressful time and so make it more likely the womb is sufficiently receptive to make assisted conception more successful.

Any of the spells in this chapter can easily be adapted to conceive an elusive subsequent child. Many are adaptations of traditional rituals from different cultures, and can also assist in pregnancy where a woman has difficulty in carrying a child to full term. Especially fortuitous times for conception are when the moon passes into Taurus and Cancer (for two and a half days each month) or when the full moon is in Taurus or Cancer.

Making a Fertility Bag, Whether You Are Trying Naturally or with Medical Intervention

YOU WILL NEED

A silver candle ✳ Three walnuts, three pearls, a small crystal egg in rose quartz or jade, a long silver pin wrapped in cloth, three orange carnelian or red jasper crystals ✳ An orange drawstring bag or purse ✳ An orange ribbon ✳ A piece of silk

TIMING

During the full moon

THE SPELL

* Light the candle, adding the walnuts, pearls, crystal egg, pin, and crystals to your bag, one by one, and say afterward, *Gabriel, angel of unborn children, and Mother Moon, send our waiting child to grow safe, within my/my partner's womb.*

* Knot the ribbon around the bag three times, saying, *Come little one to us, come soon. Angel Gabriel and Mother Moon, help our infant to grow safe, within my/my partner's womb.*

* Leave the bag on the indoor bedroom window ledge. After the full moon, keep it wrapped in silk in your bedroom.

An All-Purpose Fertility Spell

YOU WILL NEED

An oval-shaped carnelian or red jasper crystal ★ A needle
or a long silver-colored pin ★ A small, soft, pink cloth

TIMING

Three nights before and the night of the full moon

THE SPELL

* On night 1, hold the crystal in your nondominant hand, pressing the
  point of the needle against the crystal. Say, *So are we joined in love,
  and welcome our beautiful child, to add to/complete our family unity.*

* Set the crystal and needle slightly apart on the indoor bedroom
  window ledge.

* Repeat the spell for the following two nights.

* On the night of the full moon, repeat the spell words and actions,
  leaving the crystal and the needle touching on the window ledge.

* If possible, make love.

* The next morning, wrap the needle and crystal together in the knotted
  pink cloth.

* Repeat the ritual monthly for as long as necessary.

Linking with the Fertility of the Moon

YOU WILL NEED

A deep glass bowl of water

TIMING

Any night just before, during, or after the full moon

THE SPELL

* Go outside, positioning the bowl so moonlight is reflected in the water.

* If it is cloudy, light silver candles around the bowl.

* Say, *Mother Moon, I call your silver light, asking your help as you shimmer bright, To bring my infant into my/my partner's womb this night.*

* Ripple your hands in the water and shake them over your womb/genitals, saying, *I wash my hands in Mother Moon, asking you to grant fertility and soon.*

* Then say, *Lady Moon, I would no longer detain you from taking your leave, I give you thanks for blessings soon to be received.*

* Pour away the water on the ground.

To Conceive a Much-Wanted Child If You Are Getting Anxious Because Nothing Is Happening

YOU WILL NEED

A coconut, sacred to Sri, the Hindu goddess of fertility and prosperity ✳ An egg ✳ Almond or olive oil ✳ Rose essential oil

TIMING

During the crescent moon

THE SPELL

* When the moon is/should be visible, break open the coconut.

* Drink some of the coconut juice, then take half of the coconut shell and put the egg inside it.

* Sprinkle both the coconut and the egg with almond or olive oil, saying, *Mother Goddesses, through the years, have comforted their daughters' and sons' tears, offering fertility. In your sacred fruit, send a child to me.*

* Set the egg in the coconut on a river, stream, or the outgoing tide.

* Make love as soon as possible after the spell, anointing your/your partner's womb with slightly warmed almond or olive oil with a drop or two of rose essential oil mixed in.

Using Lodestones If Your Partner Is Unwilling to Have a Baby, But Parenthood Is Important to You

YOU WILL NEED

A pointed lodestone or magnetite (for a male) and a rounded lodestone (for a female); two of the same stones for a same-sex couple, or two hematites * Iron filings (magnetic sand) or rose oil * A red bag * A tiny lodestone

TIMING

Early Friday

THE SPELL

* Soak your larger lodestones in water until noon, dry them, and sprinkle iron filings or a drop of oil on each, saying, *our love is good, we two, that will never change. And if we create a me and you, close we will remain.*

* Place the lodestones in the bag.

* Repeat the spell for six days.

* On day 7, add the tiny lodestone to the bag, sprinkling sand or oil into the bag, and say, *Don't be afraid, two becoming three. For creating a new you and new me, even closer shall we be.*

* Keep the three lodestones in the bag under your mattress.

An Ancient Egyptian Mother Hathor Ritual If Either Partner Has Reproductive Problems That Make Conception Difficult

YOU WILL NEED

Modeling clay, shaped into a woman with a huge belly
and breasts, wearing a necklace ★ Modeling clay, formed into an
erect phallus shape ★ Modeling clay, shaped into a baby in a cradle,
set between the other symbols ★ Lily or lotus fragrance or oil
★ Palm or exotic green leaves ★ Red thread ★ Candles

TIMING

The hour before sunset

THE SPELL

* Anoint each of the three symbols with fragrance, saying, *By Mother Hathor, who thousands of years ago, granted children to those who made their offerings, this night remove all barriers, and a beloved child bring.*

* Wrap the symbols in the leaves, secured with red thread, and carry them and the candles to wherever you will make love.

* In the morning, roll the clay into a ball, retie the leaves, and bury them outdoors in greenery.

Making a Full Moon Fertility Charm

YOU WILL NEED

A jasmine or myrrh incense stick, in an incense holder
* A selenite, milky quartz, or moonstone crystal, or a
silver ring, bracelet, or necklace/pendant as a charm

TIMING

During the full moon, outdoors

THE SPELL

* Light the incense. Holding the charm in your
nondominant hand, draw over it in incense smoke
the triple moon image (see drawing), saying, *Mother Moon,
maternal might, fill now my/my partner's womb with fertile light.*

* Return the incense to its holder.

* Holding the charm in front of you in open, outstretched hands, whirl
around seven times counterclockwise, saying the spell words fast seven
times. Face the moon so the moon seems to rush toward you.

* Wear or carry the charm, retracing the triple moon image on its surface
with the index finger of your dominant hand, before making love.

A Viking Bind or Joining Rune Blessing, If You Have Previously Miscarried during Pregnancy

YOU WILL NEED

A thin piece of wood or a stone ★ Red paint
★ A red pen or a waterproof marker

TIMING

When you know you have conceived

THE SPELL

* On the wood or stone, in red paint, pen, or waterproof marker, combine the three runes on the right in any pattern you like: Gebo, the gift of a happy relationship and the gift of a baby; Ingwaz, the father god; and Berkano, the mother goddess, or use my pattern below.

* Say, as you draw or paint, softly and continuously, *Bind the babe safe within, until the right time to be born. Safe in blessings, wrapped in love, healthy, strong, to greet his/her birthday morn.*

* Hang your bind rune where morning light shines and touch it at night and in the morning until you feel more confident about the pregnancy, repeating the spell words.

GEBO

INGWAZ,
THE FATHER GOD

BERKANO,
THE MOTHER
GODDESS

A St. Anne Beeswax Ritual If You Are Trying to Conceive a Child Later in Life in a New or Existing Relationship

YOU WILL NEED

Two beeswax candles, side by side on a metal tray
∗ Herb ∗ Yellow roses ∗ A thin screwdriver or
letter opener ∗ A piece of white silk

TIMING

Friday, the day of Anne, saint of beekeepers and grandmother of Jesus

THE SPELL

∗ Light the left-hand candle and sprinkle a little herb in the flame, saying,
Anne, in later years you mother became. We ask for a child in your name.

∗ Repeat the spell words and actions for the second candle

∗ In the pool of wax between the candles, sprinkle rose petals, saying,
*In our hearts we still are young, But we can offer wisdom too.
Babe of our middle years, All our life through.*

∗ In the cooling wax, with the screwdriver, draw a baby in a cradle,
cut it out, and wrap it in white silk.

∗ Make love.

If You Are Having a Baby Alone, Whether by Choice or as a Single Parent

YOU WILL NEED

A pink rose each month * A picture of you as a baby and
any ultrasound images of your baby on top * Nine pearls
* A glass jar * A red rose bush for a boy and a white one for a girl

TIMING

Monthly until the birth

THE SPELL

* Put a single rose petal on top of the picture(s), saying, *Always beloved will you be, we are already a united family.*

* Put a pearl in the jar, saying, *Precious as a pearl shall you be, we are already a united family.*

* Pluck and scatter all the rose petals.

* Repeat the spell each month.

* After the birth or if you reunite with or meet someone new during the pregnancy, shake the pearl jar, saying, *Should anyone join our family, they will need to love both you and me.*

* After the birth, plant a red rose bush for a boy and a white one for a girl.

If You Are Using a Donor or Surrogate, Whether for Medical Reasons, Because You Are a Same-Sex Couple, or Are Transgendered

139

YOU WILL NEED

Three identical small rose quartz crystals
* A well-washed, drained egg, from which you have cut a lid
* Red tape or sealing wax * Brightly colored pens

TIMING

One to two weeks before the implantation

THE SPELL

* Place the rose quartz crystals in the eggshell, cradle the eggshell in your hands, and say, *My love* [Name partner], *this is our very own baby to be, in soul and spirit and in unity. We take thankfully the seed/egg of s/he, who quickens life for you and me.*

* Seal the egg with tape or sealing wax and carefully decorate the shell with spirals, flowers, and swirls.

* Keep it safe until after the successful birth, and bury the egg and its contents beneath a thriving rose or lavender bush.

For a Safe and Healthy Pregnancy and Birth at Full Term

YOU WILL NEED

A red cord ★ A drawstring bag for the cord ★ Flowers

TIMING

When you know you are pregnant

THE SPELL

* Tie three loose knots in the cord, saying as you tie each one, *Baby keep safe within, until your right time for birth begins. Then come easily, healthfully, joyously, welcomed by your waiting family.*

* Put the knotted cord in the bag and touch the knots whenever you feel anxious during pregnancy, repeating the spell words.

* When labor begins and/or you go to the hospital or birthing center, untie the first knot, saying, *Baby, your time has come, to enter the world. Come easily and safely, to your waiting family.*

* Untie the second and third knots as labor progresses or before any medical intervention.

* When you go home, decorate the cord with flowers, hanging it on a special tree you buy for the baby.

A Celtic Blessing to Welcome
Your Baby into the World

YOU WILL NEED

Pure water, if possible from a sacred well, or holy water

TIMING

After you come home from the hospital or birthing center

THE SPELL

* Anoint the center of the baby's forehead with a drop of pure water, saying, *By earth and sea and sky, be blessed.*

* Anoint the center of the baby's brow, saying, *By moon and stars and sun, be sanctified.*

* Anoint next the baby's wrists, first left then right, saying, *May you never be hungry, never be thirsty, never cry alone. And may the angels protect you, as you sleep and wake.*

* Finally, carry the baby upstairs to the top of the stairs, saying, *Rise in life in prosperity, success, love and happiness. And do good to all creatures, of the earth, sea, and skies.*

* If you do not have stairs, gently lift the baby upward, cradled in your arms.

A Spell to Bond with a Newborn Infant after a Difficult Birth or If There Are Complications

Note: This is one that may be helpful to share with the other parent.

YOU WILL NEED
Yourself

TIMING
When the baby is asleep

THE SPELL

* Touch the center of your brow and then your infant's brow, saying, *We are joined spirit to spirit, soul to soul. I will always do my best, when you wake and when you rest.*

* Touch your own closed lips and then the infant's. Say, *We are joined breath to breath, to being a mother/father I am new, and this world is strange to you. But together shall we learn, to love each other, me and you.*

* Finally, touch your heart and then the infant's, and say, *We are joined heart and heart. So shall it be always, even when we are apart. I will not leave you till you're grown, and have a family of your own.*

* Repeat the ritual whenever you start to feel overwhelmed, as most parents do by a new baby.

For One Last Try at IVF or Another Form of Medical Intervention

YOU WILL NEED
Three Chinese divinatory coins

TIMING
Before a final treatment

THE SPELL

* Shake the three coins in your closed hands and toss them onto a table, without looking at them. Say, *Going for success, one last try. bring us good fortune, the stakes are high.*

* Shake and toss the coins again, saying, *Risking all, on this final call. A child we seek. One last throw, no reason why it should not be so.*

* Shake and toss them a final time, saying, *Winner takes all, success do I call. We cannot, we shall not, fail or fall.*

* Outside the treatment center, throw the coins as far as you can away from you, saying, *Our fate I cast to the winds. Return as happiness, so the loser wins.*

CHAPTER 10

Sex Magick

S ex magick is one of the most beautiful, spiritual, and potent forms of love magick. It enhances lovemaking when this has become routine. It is also a very powerful way for two people to release energy for a joint desire or need, and is one of the most powerful forms of spell-casting.

Over time you will create with your partner your own unique, beautiful, and spiritual forms of sex magick, both to strengthen your love and to release energies for specific purposes in the everyday world.

Sex magick is effective even without a partner, especially if you begin with a symbolic sex ceremony. You can set the scene as noted in the different spells and say the words in your mind during lovemaking, releasing your wishes or desires into the cosmos as you reach orgasm. Sex magick traditionally takes place in outdoor settings, but you can easily rent a secluded cottage or take a tent into the wilderness for the weekend.

Finally, you can use sex magick if you feel you are ready to make love in a relationship, but your partner is reluctant to do so.

The first two spells are longer than most of those found in this book, as they are the most significant and traditional in sex magick and can be used as a prelude to sex magick or as the basis for creating your own sex magick spells.

Sex Magic to Release Power to Obtain Specific Needs and Wishes

Note: You can do this ritual during lovemaking by saying the words in your head if your partner would be reluctant to do so.

YOU WILL NEED

Sandalwood or ylang-ylang essential oil
* Rose-, lotus-, or lily-scented candles

TIMING

During the full moon

THE SPELL

* Add sandalwood or ylang-ylang to your bathwater/shower, lighting candles around the bath (share the bath with your partner, if you wish).

* Carry the candles to the bedroom unless you make love in the bath or shower.

* Sit on the bed, not touching but breathing as one.

* Begin to chant softly your most precious desires and dreams, then faster and more intensely as lovemaking progresses, matching the rhythm of the words with the movement of your bodies.

* Use the precise moment of orgasm to call out nine times the wish and then cry, *All we desire now is free.*

The Symbolic Joining of Two People through the Ancient Holy Grail Ritual to Pledge Fidelity or to Initiate Sacred Lovemaking

Note: If you're alone, take both parts. Though the ritual is written for a man and a woman, like all the spells in the book, it works just as well for a same-sex couple with very little if any modification of words or actions.

YOU WILL NEED

A goblet or a crystal glass with a stem, filled with water or wine, representing the traditional grail cup ✳ A piece of smoothed wood, pointed at one end as a wand, a crystal massage wand, or a silver-colored knife, representing the sacred lance or spear ✳ Two white candles, with the wand to the right of them and the glass to the left

TIMING

Late at night

THE SPELL

* Light the candle at left and have your partner light the candle at right in total silence.

* Take the cup between your hands, raising it in turn over each of the candles and sit or kneel, holding it.

* Your partner now takes the wand in his right hand, holding it, point downward, in turn over each candle.

* You, holding the cup, drink from it, then offer it to your partner's lips so he can drink.

* Your partner raises the wand above the cup and you ask, *Whom does the sacred grail lance serve?*

* Your partner replies, *You, my lady, for evermore, I dedicate to you, my power and my protection.*

* Raise the chalice so that the point of the wand is almost touching and your partner asks, *Whom does the sacred grail cup heal?*

* You answer, *You, my lord, for evermore, I dedicate to you, my love and my fertility.*

* Finally, your partner slowly plunges the lance into the wine nine times, saying, *So are we joined in love eternally,* and you both make pledges of love and fidelity to each other.

* If you wish, afterward gently make love.

* Leave the candles to burn through.

A Viking Runic Sex Magick Ritual to Bind Your Love to You If Sex Has Become Routine

YOU WILL NEED

A red, nonsmear lipstick or face-paint
stick ∗ Three red candles, in a row

TIMING

Before making love

THE SPELL

∗ Draw with lipstick or a face-paint stick one of the runes,
as soon on the right, on each unlit candle.

∗ Light the red candles in a row in the bedroom, saying
(in your mind if necessary), *By the power of the Vikings,
ecstasy this night shall fire. Burn runes. Release your
unquenchable passion, powerful with desire.*

∗ In lipstick, adorn your breasts, your womb, and your
inner thighs with the runic symbols and your partner's
outer thighs, navel, and just above the genitals, saying,
Naudhiz, Kenaz, and Thurisaz, flame and fire within.

∗ Make love and maybe consider one of the symbols
as a tattoo.

NAUDHIZ, THE FIRE
OF PASSION

KENAZ, THE BLAZING
TORCH OF UNQUENCHABLE
SEXUAL DESIRE

THURISAZ, THE HAMMER
OF POTENCY AND SEXUAL
ECSTASY OF THOR

If Your Male Partner Betrays You and Thinks You Don't Know

YOU WILL NEED

A large unpeeled banana * A sharp knife

TIMING

Before you meet

THE SPELL

* Stroke the banana from top to bottom continuously, talking erotically and seductively to your faithless partner.

* Gently remove the peel and toss it over your left shoulder, saying, *Slipped up, didn't you? Promised to be true. But you got caught out, and I won't shout, but just get rid of you.*

* Chop up the banana and eat it. Dispose of the peel and, if you wish, the lover.

If Your Female Partner Betrays
You and You Find Out

YOU WILL NEED

Six oysters in their shells or, alternatively, six
strawberries * An oyster knife or an ordinary knife

TIMING

When you find out

THE SPELL

* Stroke the sides of each oyster shell or caress the strawberries, describing
  an erotic moment you shared.

* Pry out each oyster in turn, swallowing it whole, or cut off the tops of
  the strawberries one by one and bite into them hard.

* Then say, *Thought I was a fool, you broke every rule, of fidelity and
  loyalty. Now you're gone, romancing with you is done.*

* Get out and start socializing.

An Ancient Egyptian Fragrance Sex Ritual to Call a Hesitant Lover to Your Bed

YOU WILL NEED

A bowl and a spoon * Rose petals from a fragrant red
rose * Dried cinnamon * Nine pubic hairs * Lotus
or papyrus perfume oil * Orange candles

TIMING

During the full moon

THE SPELL

* Mix in a bowl with the spoon the petals and cinnamon, add the hairs and burn a little of the mix outdoors, saying, *The flowers burn, like my passion untamed. I call you in fragrance and in flame. This night in love we shall entwine, you shall be mine.*

* Bury half of the mix under any tree inside a leaf.

* Add six drops of oil to the remainder, putting it in your bedroom.

* Light orange candles and call your love aloud, using any excuse.

* Anoint your bedsheets and yourself with the oil before s/he arrives.

Another Ancient Egyptian Incense Spell for Beautiful Sex and Past Life Visions

YOU WILL NEED

Four lighted orange candles, one in each corner of a room ✳ Four lighted frankincense or myrrh incense sticks, one in each corner

TIMING

At sunset

THE SPELL

✳ Lie together in candlelight, inhaling the incense and saying as a chant words adapted from an ancient Egyptian prayer to love: *The fire is laid, the fire shines. The incense is laid on the fire, the incense shines. Your perfume comes to me, O Incense, I dedicate myself on this altar of love, to my love and s/he to me. This night by candlelight, we join our love to when first I did see you, first know, surely eons ago.*

✳ As you make love, you may have visions of other worlds where you were once together.

A Cerne Abbas Fertility and Potency Ritual to Conceive a Child or to Spice Up Your Sex Life

YOU WILL NEED

A small tray of earth and very small white stones to mark the outline * Seeds of fast-growing herbs

TIMING

At dawn

THE SPELL

* Mark the outline of a phallic figure like the one below and plant it with the fast-growing seeds.

* Name the person with whom you wish to have a child or increase passion, saying, *May we be fruitful/know true ecstasy in our love.*

* Leave the tray outside from dawn to noon and then keep it in a sheltered place.

* Cut the herbs when ready, serving them as part of a special meal for the two of you before lovemaking.

Ancient chalk figures such as the Cerne Abbas Giant have traditionally been regarded as powerful potency figures.

CHAPTER 11

Spells to Enchant and Break Enchantments around You and Your Lover, Caused by Temptation or Negative Magick

Enchanting a lover is a magical technique that involves increasing your aura radiance through spells so that someone you like a lot suddenly realizes that you could be the real person of his/her dreams. If your partner is taking you for granted, an enchantment spell will put you right there, center stage.

Enchantment can be a double-edged sword and, in an established relationship, however loving, it's possible that someone will make a play for your partner. In this case, spells can protect your partner from being enchanted and weaken any enchantments when you suspect your partner or potential partner is obsessed.

Finally, if you are tempted, but regret it afterward, spells can assist in breaking the bewitchment you know will destroy a basically sound relationship in exchange for a few nights of passion.

This chapter also deals with the more serious aspect of nasty exes or jealous relatives who have used black magick against you. Some of the spells here protect against hexes (formal spells cast against your relationship) or vicious, spoken curses that can cause conflicts in your relationship or persistent misfortune that makes it hard to be happy.

However, if your partner is a serial cheat, though spells may paper over the problem, ultimately you may want to consider if the relationship is right for you or you should find a more trustworthy partner.

An All-Purpose Enchantment Rite
to Entrance a New Love

YOU WILL NEED

An amethyst, fluorite, or opal, ideally on a pendant

TIMING

At the beginning of a month

THE SPELL

* Make hand contact with the desired person; for example, offering a cup of coffee and saying silently, *The link is made, our essences blend. This is the beginning, may there be no end.*

* As soon as practical, touch your heart with the same hand, then touch the crystal, doing this six times.

* Put the crystal on a flat surface. Moving your dominant hand clockwise and the other hand counterclockwise at the same time a few inches above the crystal, say softly, *I enchant you. When you look at me, entranced will you be. Spellbound, me alone will you see.*

* Wear or carry the crystal. Whenever you meet, touch the crystal.

To Enchant Someone Who Doesn't Seem to Notice You except as a Friend or Colleague

YOU WILL NEED

Something s/he has touched, preferably with her/his lips, such as a coffee cup, a glass, or a pen ★ Two small pieces of white silk ★ Two yellow flowers in soil, traditionally marigolds

TIMING

As soon as possible after the touch, somewhere private

THE SPELL

200

* Wipe the item all over with one piece of silk, saying, *So your essence do I capture. Look at me with love's own rapture.*

* Now do the same with a cup you have used.

* Wash the two pieces of silk in a small bowl of cold water together, repeating the spell words.

* Pour some water from the bowl onto the flowers, saying, *Look at me through the eyes of ecstasy. Spellbound together may we be.*

* Care for your flowers, making an extra effort to be noticed positively by the unobservant object of your desire.

A Traditional Fey Enchantment Ritual to Make You Irresistible to a Known or yet Unknown Person

YOU WILL NEED:

Seven small silver candles * A mirror * Two 2-pointed white selenite crystals or pointed clear quartz crystals

TIMING

During the full moon

THE SPELL

* Light the silver candles around the mirror and face the mirror.

* Holding one crystal in each hand, breathe three times, first on the left-hand crystal and then the right-hand one.

* Then say, *May my light shine forth gloriously, to draw to me love irresistibly, by the power of the fey. Wind and bind enchantment in, weave, bright as moonglow, shimmering gold, fairy glamour I unfold.*

* Raise your arms over your head and spiral the crystals all around your head and shoulders, not quite touching, in a steady rhythm. Repeat the spell words softly and slowly, until you feel the magick within you.

* Blow out the candles fast.

An Oil Ritual to Enchant Your Lover with Passion

202

YOU WILL NEED

A rose-scented candle * A dish of slightly warmed
lotus, rose, or chamomile essential oil,
diluted in sweet almond oil

TIMING

Before you meet

THE SPELL

* Light the candle in the bedroom, passing the dish of fragrance above the flame, and say, *I seek this night pure enchantment and bliss.*

* Anoint with a single drop of fragrance the center of your forehead, saying, *I am the lotus, that comes from fields of everlasting light. Fill me with love and passion this night.*

* Anoint the middle of your brow, the base of your throat, between your breasts or the center of your chest, the center of your upper stomach, your navel, and, finally, the top of each inner thigh, each time repeating the spell words.

* Finally, hold the dish over the candle once more, saying, *Enchantment burns within me. Irresistible and unresisting shall I be.*

Adding Color to Your Oil Enchantment Ritual

Seven candles—red, orange, yellow, green, blue, indigo or
purple, and white—in a semicircle in the bedroom where you
will anoint yourself ✻ A dish of slightly warmed lotus, rose,
or chamomile essential oil, diluted in sweet almond oil

TIMING

Before anointing yourself

THE SPELL

* Light the red candle, pass the dish of fragrance above the flame, saying,
  I seek this night pure enchantment and bliss. Blaze scarlet passion fire.

* Light the orange candle, repeating the spell actions and words, but
  substituting *Blaze orange with desire.*

* For the yellow candle, substitute *Blaze yellow with ecstasy*; for the green
  candle, *blaze with fidelity*; for the blue candle, *blaze that love will always
  be true*; for indigo/purple, *blaze as we fly*; and for white, *and passion
  reaches the sky.*

* Begin the anointing, as in the previous spell.

* When you know your partner better, you can share the ritual and
  incorporate the oil, or one your partner likes for intimate massage.

A Secret-Word Spell to Enchant
a Reluctant or Slow Lover

YOU WILL NEED
A long red thread

TIMING
At the end of the moon cycle

THE SPELL

* Tie nine knots in the thread, left to right, saying, *Nine by nine, I would make you mine. Enchanted shall you be. Give me a sign, that you care for me.*

* As you touch each knot, left to right, create secret words of enchantment that you will say in your mind when you meet, while talking about ordinary things, and looking into your lover's eyes as you speak. For example, your secret words might be, *Be for me, a lover true. Enchanted, spellbound, ecstatic be. Enraptured as you speak to me.*

* Wear the knotted thread, pinned inside your clothes, when you meet.

An All-Purpose Breaking Enchantment Ritual

A dark purple cord or strong thread ✶ Scissors
or a sharp knife ✶ A paper bag

TIMING

*When you need to break a destructive love enchantment
against you or your partner*

THE SPELL

* Tie nine loose knots, right to left, in the cord, saying, *Though held
in thrall, these knots will release all.*

* From right to left, cut off each knot and drop it in a paper bag, saying,
Enchantment so you lose your sway, fascination forever cut away.

* Take the bag of knots and throw it into an outdoor trash can without a
lid, saying, *Cleared from* [Name] *and from me, tossed away and so to stay.*

Creating a Psychic Exclusion Zone If You Know Your Partner Is Easily Led Astray

YOU WILL NEED

A picture of the two of you ✳ Something your partner carries almost all the time—a credit card holder, a phone, or keys ✳ A dragon's blood or frankincense incense stick ✳ A bowl of water

TIMING

The night before the crescent moon

THE SPELL

* Put the picture under the item your partner carries, saying, *Together bound in love are we, whenever you touch* [name the item], *think only of me. To your heart I alone have the key.*

* Light the incense. Hold it like a smoke pen and draw smoke keys around the picture and item, saying, *The key I hold to your heart. None shall lead you astray when we are apart.*

* Plunge the incense stick, lighted end down, in the water. As it dries, draw with the incense stick on the back of the picture your initials enclosed in a key.

If You Gave in to Temptation and Want to Forget It Ever Happened

An old ceramic pot ∗ A red ceramic pen
or permanent marker ∗ Musk incense sticks

TIMING

The day after the lapse

THE SPELL

∗ Write on the pot in red, NO THROUGH ROAD, THE WAY IS BARRED.
THIS ENCHANTMENT I BREAK, FOR EVERYONE'S SAKE.

∗ Say the spell words as you cover the writing in red.

∗ Light the incense sticks in the pot, saying, *Covering my tracks, for
everyone's sake, the price was high, and there's no going back. Incense
obscure, in mist this mistake. For one night of excitement, my relationship
I won't break.*

∗ Smash the pot and dispose of the shards and the contents, saying,
*I got burned, but sense I've learned. This enchantment I break,
for everyone's sake.*

If Your Partner Makes Exciting New Friends or Finds His/Her Colleagues Fascinating, and Treats You Like a Piece of Furniture

YOU WILL NEED

A toy jack-in-the-box or a wind-up toy, plus a small box to fit it

TIMING

When you get excluded yet again

THE SPELL

* Pop up the jack-in-the-box or the wind-up the toy, saying fast, *Jack-in-the-box, up you pop, and out you drop, from my life, to your spellbinding new friends. To you I'm merely part of the furniture or faded wallpaper. You take what you need and off you caper. But this shall end.*

* Slam the jack-in-the-box shut or close the toy in the box, saying, *Break the enchantment, break the connection. You're drawn nowhere now, except my direction.*

* Put the box away.

If Your Longtime Partner Suddenly Reverts to Adolescent Behavior and Tells You That You Are No Fun

YOU WILL NEED

A picture of a clown ✳ A red pen

TIMING

After your partner has gone out with his/her friends

THE SPELL

✳ Write all over the picture in red, [NAME], STOP ACTING LIKE A CLOWN.

✳ Moving both your hands over the picture counterclockwise nine times, say nine times, *I disenchant you, stop playing the clown. This new you I really hate. I will break the spell, before it's too late.*

✳ Turn around fast nine times counterclockwise, holding the picture, and say, *I take off your blinkers of false youth. Grow up fast, shed this delusion, give up illusion. This warning is your last.*

✳ Shred the clown picture and flush the pieces down the toilet with lots of drain cleaner.

A Spell to Banish a Vamp or Lothario Who Is Threatening an Otherwise Happy Relationship

YOU WILL NEED

Three red candles of descending size, set left to right ★ A long pin or needle ★ A cheese grater

TIMING

On three consecutive nights

THE SPELL

* On night 1, hold the largest unlit candle, saying softly and continuously, *Begone from our lives, false fire. I must be your only desire.*

* Light the largest candle and only for a second hold the pin (carefully or with tongs) in the flame, saying, *Burn away, turn away, this enchantment be snuffed out. Grow cold like this flame, the end of your game.*

* Extinguish the largest candle.

* On the second and third nights, repeat the spell with the other two candles.

* Shred the three candles with a cheese grater.

* Each day after the spell is completed, sprinkle a little shredded wax outside your premises or his/her vehicle until it is all gone.

An Enchantment Breaker to Deter Your Partner, Who Is Being Lured to a Single Neighbor or Friend's Home Too Often

Note: If the threat is at work, you can do this near the workplace.

YOU WILL NEED

Two long twigs from a thornbush or a prickly tree ⋆ A fabric bag ⋆ Dried nettles from a health store or split tea bags

TIMING

Early in the day

THE SPELL

* Overnight, put the twigs in the bag with the nettles.

* Shake the bag well, saying, *Sharp the pain of this enchantment, being helpful you may be. But it's not the need for your good deeds, I see, my amorous missionary.*

* Go to a path or entrance your partner uses on the mercy missions to the friend's/neighbor's premises.

* Cross and hide the twigs, scattering the nettles on the ground nearby.

* Say, [Name your partner], *do not enter here. Common sense you lack. The enchantment is broken, the words spoken, to this place you cannot come back.*

Breaking a Hex or Negative Enchantment on Your Relationship by an Ex-Partner, a Relative, or a Paid Practitioner

YOU WILL NEED

Two black feathers ✻ String

TIMING

On the last day of the waning moon

THE SPELL

✳ With a feather in each hand, go into every room of your home, brushing doors and windows with the feathers, and say, *I remove your enchantment from this place. No more in our relationship shall your evil show its face.*

✳ On the ground floor, go to the front door (you can do this in an upstairs apartment), cross the feathers, and then uncross them, in the center, inside and outside, saying, *Uncrossed, your power is lost.*

✳ Take the feathers from the house. Tie them with string to a dying tree, saying, *Evil enchantment blow away, from our lives forever stay. Returned is the hex with all its pain, and it cannot come back again.*

If a Family Member or an Ex-Partner Has Cursed Your Relationship

213

YOU WILL NEED

A sharp knife ✴ A lemon ✴ A deep bowl
of salt ✴ Two leafless twigs

TIMING

Wednesday morning

THE SPELL

* With the sharp knife, cut the lemon in half and press the two halves of the lemon, fruit side down, in the salt bowl, saying, *Dry all life from this enchantment, evil words and wishes meant. As you wither so dies the curse, you did your worst, come not again.*

* Leave the bowl where the sun shines.

* When the lemons are totally dried out, remove them from the salt and, if possible, bury them near the perpetrator's home or, if not buried, well away from your home with two crossed leafless twigs on top, saying, *Your curse has seeped away, dried up, withered, decayed. Never again can it be made.*

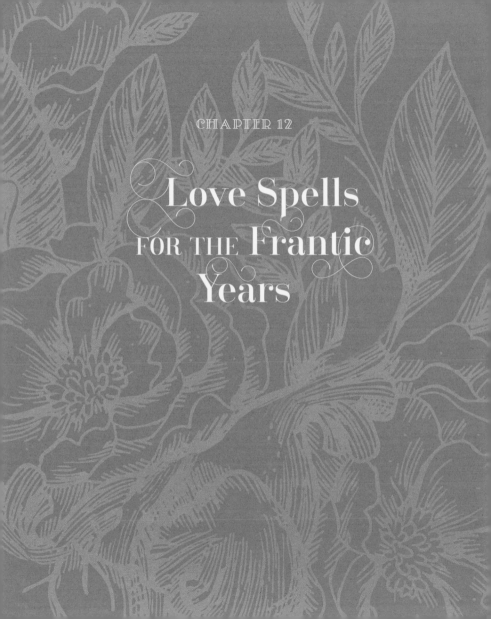

CHAPTER 12

Love Spells
FOR THE Frantic
Years

Our twenties through to our early forties are years of constant juggling that can make forging and maintaining relationships hard— finding the right partner or starting over in love, perhaps with small children if a relationship goes wrong. Love can be pushed onto the back burner in the frantic juggle of daily demands.

The spells in this chapter will create or re-create a magical space to find or reclaim love and to avoid becoming two trains on separate tracks, following sometimes conflicting career demands, where romantic conversations are replaced by worries over the bills and deciding whose turn it is to drop the children off at school. They can reignite that flagging ego and fill your energy field with light and charisma. And if you are alone, or in an unhappy relationship, not only can you attract the right person, but you may be instinctively drawn to the right place at the right time to meet him/her.

Finally, you may feel that everyone has a stake in your love life—interfering parents and in-laws, friends who resent that you can no longer stay out until 3 A.M., and employers who make impossible demands that encroach on precious and scarce leisure time. Spells can give you much-needed breathing room for yourself and your partner in the midst of this hectic time in your lives.

If Your Partner Wants You to Stay Home with the Children, but You Crave a Career and Adult Company

YOU WILL NEED

A children's playhouse or make one with a blanket
and two chairs * A feather duster * An apron

TIMING

Anytime, with or without your children

THE SPELL

* Crouch in the playhouse with your duster, wearing the apron. Dust all around, saying, *Playing house, I'm no mouse. I need relief, from talking fairy tales, poop, and teeth.*

* Climb out and dust the outside of the playhouse, saying, *Locked away in my gilded cage, for me and the kids is no advantage. They need quality, not resentful me. So, duster down, I set us free.*

* Shake the duster outdoors, saying, *Vacancy, left by escapee.*

* Put the duster and apron in the playhouse or the children's toy chest, and explore job opportunities and child care while the spell energies are still strong.

If the Family Has Taken over Your Wedding Arrangements and Turned It into a Circus

Peppercorns ∗ A picture of a society or
royal wedding ∗ Glue ∗ A cut-out picture of the
figures of you and your partner holding hands

TIMING

When you feel like eloping

THE SPELL

218

∗ Sprinkle peppercorns over the society wedding picture, saying, *Bridesmaids galore, ushers even more, meringue frocks, big hats, the wedding's no longer ours at all.*

∗ Scatter the peppercorns outdoors, saying, *Off it goes, or we'll elope, a ceremony on a beach or on a ski slope. Stop, step back, give us space. Or we'll marry wearing garbage sacks, and not a trace of lace.*

∗ Glue your images on top of the society wedding picture, saying, *Our show, our day, we'll fix it our way. Either you accept, or away you can stay.*

∗ Go for what you want.

When Children Are Ruining Your Sex Life and You Can't Get Time Away Alone

YOU WILL NEED

Two jars of garlic salt * A small bowl of rose or lavender water * A cedar or pine incense stick

TIMING

When the children are asleep

THE SPELL

* In the bedroom, set a jar of sealed garlic salt on either side of the door, saying, *Little monsters stay asleep. The garlic repels so into our bed you won't creep.*

* Sprinkle rose water on both sides of the bedroom doorknob, saying, *Sweet fragrance, bring heaven, not hell. That when we lock the door, outside you won't yell.*

* Finally, light the incense. Using it as a pen, draw three smoke doors around yours, child high, saying, *These are magical defensive doors. So you'll stay content and won't till morning roar.*

* Extinguish the incense, enjoying a night of unbridled love.

When You Have Tried Everything
to Find a Partner

YOU WILL NEED

A four-leaf clover (obtainable online) ⋆ A silver horseshoe
charm ⋆ Two magnets ⋆ Allspice ⋆ Candied angelica
⋆ Dried orange peel ⋆ Vanilla pods ⋆ Nine hairs
from your head ⋆ A green drawstring bag or purse
⋆ Three green aventurine crystals ⋆ Three green amazonites

TIMING

During a full moon night when the moon is shining

THE SPELL

* Work by moonlight, saying, *Lady Moon, bring true love soon. In vain,
  I have waited, tried and berated my ill fortune. Send love now, before
  it's too late.*

* When you have placed all the ingredients, except the crystals, in the bag,
  close the bag.

* Go outdoors, turning fast in counterclockwise circles until you feel dizzy
  and the moon seems to rush toward you, saying, *Lady Moon, I take in
  your power. I call to my love, at this hour. Find me and swiftly.*

* Keep the bag under your bed, surrounded by the crystals.

When You and Your Partner Have to Temporarily Live with Parents (Yours or His/Hers), and You Feel Suffocated

YOU WILL NEED

A special item for your private space
* Six small candles

TIMING

Weekly

THE SPELL

* Hold the item to your heart. Say, *Home is where the heart is. You, love, hold my heart. Within this* [name item], *our love is contained, as long as here we must remain.*

* Set the item in the center of the room. Light six small candles around it in a circle, blowing softly in each, then say, *With welcome, warm this place. Though the space is small, yet it is ours alone, and it our home we call.*

* Leave the candles to burn through. When you feel crowded, go to your room, hold the item, and repeat all the spell words.

* Light a green candle weekly next to it, having held it to your heart.

If You and Your Partner Want Your Own Home More Than Anything, but It Seems like an Impossible Dream

A blue candle ★ Six feathers ★ A picture of the kind of home you are striving to rent or buy, surrounded by the feathers

TIMING

Six consecutive days

THE SPELL

* Light the candle. Two by two, spiral the feathers over the picture in all directions, saying, *Dreams are many, miracles few. Yet I call our home to me and you. Let our dream become reality, bringing the home that will become our sanctuary.*

* When the candle is burned through, take one feather outdoors and release it, repeating the spell words.

* Do this each day until the feathers are gone. On the last day you will only spiral one feather.

* Wait a week, then repeat the spell. Continue until, against all hope and logic, the right home becomes available within your means.

If You Are a Single Parent with Young Children and You Want a New Partner

Two long green ribbons or cords ∗ Green thread ∗ Small dolls, representing each child ∗ Two larger dolls, one representing you and one representing a new partner ∗ Small bells

TIMING

When you meet someone new or decide to get back in the dating game

THE SPELL

* With one of the ribbons, using thread, attach each of the children's dolls to each other, then attach your doll to theirs.

* Between each doll tie a bell, saying, *We are one family, unity, my children and me. Whoever can love us all, may join our family.*

* Ring each bell in turn.

* Attach the doll representing your future love on the second ribbon, joining that ribbon to yours, and say, *Join our family, loving us equally.*

* Ring the bells and repeat the spell words.

* Hang the ribbons and dolls inside the front door.

223

If Your Partner Doesn't Know How to Share Money or Your Attention

YOU WILL NEED

Ingredients for a cake you will make
* Sugar violets for generosity, cinnamon for abundance, dried fruits, and rose essence for trust

TIMING

Before friends come for tea

THE SPELL

* Mix the cake batter, saying, *I blend in generosity, the more that is offered, the more there will be. Open your heart, my love. Life share and dare.*

* Blend in sugar violets, cinnamon, dried fruits, and rose essence, saying, *Abundance shared is twice as sweet, spread as trust equally.* [Name], *reach out, my love, willingly.*

* When the cake is baked, share it equally, saying in your mind as you offer a slice to your partner, *Don't store up love for a rainy tomorrow, leave behind old fears and sorrow. As you eat, share life's pleasures. Learn to give, not squirrel love's treasures.*

When You Both Have the Chance to Travel, But Your Partner Wants to Settle Down

YOU WILL NEED

A bowl of colored sand * A bowl of small crystal chips

TIMING

During the waxing moon

THE SPELL

* Run your hands through the sand, saying, *The sands of time are not running out, years we have to save and plan. Let's not turn away opportunity, come explore the world with me.*

* Add crystal chips to the bowl, saying, *So many adventures, so many places, Magical cities, open spaces. The world can be ours, endless possibility on us showers. Reach out, don't doubt.*

* Shake the bowl and scatter the crystalline sand in an open place, saying, *When we are older, sensible shall we be. Scrimping, saving, and planning, our priority. But we are still young, the sands of time soon gone. So reach out for joyous adventure with me.*

When Your Love Is Too Comfortable at Home to Move In with You Full Time

YOU WILL NEED

A small clay figure, representing your lover * An ornamental raffia nest or shallow basket * A soft lining for the nest * A bush

TIMING

After yet another excuse

THE SPELL

* Set the figure in the nest, outdoors perched in a bush.

* Rock the nest gently, crooning, *Rock-a-bye, big baby, secure in your nest. You love your mom's cooking, and your clothes washed and pressed.*

* Rock a little harder, saying, *Rock-a-bye, big baby, the world's a tough place. You like to be cosseted, and everything in place.*

* Rock even harder, throwing the figure out of the nest, and say, *Rock-a-bye, baby bird, time you were flown. Come live with me soon, or you'll end up alone.*

* Hang the empty nest in the bush, rolling the figure into a ball.

* Issue an ultimatum.

When Your Partner Has Secrets

Four roses—one white, one pink, one red,
and one yellow ✳ A vase

TIMING

Saturday

THE SPELL

✳ Pluck all the petals from the white rose and scatter them outdoors,
saying, *Secrecy no more shall be. Honest and open now be with me.*

✳ Pluck half the petals from the pink rose and scatter them in the same
place, saying, *Step by step and piece by piece, your secrets shall you release.*

✳ Pluck a quarter of the petals from the red rose, saying, *True love built
on openness and trust, whatever your secrets, share them we must.*

✳ Put the pink and red rose in the vase.

✳ Hold the yellow rose and say, *Love will last throughout the years, sharing
laughter and also tears. No secrets between us, shall there be, but honesty,
trust, and fidelity.*

✳ Add the yellow rose to the vase.

When Your Partner Isn't Doing His/ Her Fair Share of the Chores or Taking Responsibility for Family Life

YOU WILL NEED

A string puppet

TIMING

During the waxing moon

THE SPELL

* Make the puppet dance, so the feet aren't touching the ground, and say, *Lazy Bones, you make me groan. You dance to your own tune. Or join whoever seems more fun, you just don't get there's a home to run.*

* Drop the strings so the figure flops on the floor, saying, *Lazy Bones, you make me groan. Stop nagging me you say. But only because of the chores I do, can you go out to play.*

* Cut one of the strings, saying, *From now on, Lazy Bones, from me no more groans. Stand on your own two feet, real life you're going to head-on meet.*

* Go on strike, doing no more chores, repair the string, and give the puppet to a child who will enjoy playing with it.

When You Want Another Baby,
But Your Partner Does Not

YOU WILL NEED

A square drawn in red on white paper to represent the
existing family, with one side of the square missing
* Within the square, set a rose quartz crystal for every existing
family member, plus one outside for the unborn family member

TIMING

During the full moon

THE SPELL

* Add the unborn baby crystal to the others inside the square, shaking
them in your cupped hands, and say ten times, *May our family be blessed,
if right for all, with a new addition, that we may share the joy of completion.
Take away doubt, take away fear, that all will rejoice once the missing
one's here.*

* Draw in the missing line, repeating the spell words ten more times.

* Repeat the spell weekly with a new sheet of paper and the same crystals
until your partner changes his/her mind.

When Your Partner Gets Cold Feet and Calls Off the Wedding or Engagement, But Still Wants to Be Part of Your Life

YOU WILL NEED

A broken necklace, or loose beads and a string, in a dish

TIMING

When your partner acts as if nothing has changed

THE SPELL

* Shake the dish, saying, *Least said, soonest mended, but not if your dreams have ended. We can't go on as before. Fix this mess or walk out of the door.*

* Start to string the beads.

* When you have finished, hold the necklace over the dish, but don't tie the string, saying, *What's it to be? Come back to me? Commitment instantly must I see.*

* Let the beads fall into the dish, restring the necklace, tie it, and say, *Lifelong fidelity, nothing less. Or my necklace and I will seek new happiness.*

When You Are Constantly Told You That Have to Choose between Your Partner and Your Family

231

YOU WILL NEED

A blue candle ★ A piece of string with a bead in the middle

TIMING

After another dispute

THE SPELL

* Light the candle and hold the string so the bead veers from end to end, saying, *Tug-of-war, I'm the bone you're fighting for.*

* Continue but slow down the movement, saying, *Which to choose, either way I lose.*

* Take the bead off the string, saying, *I love you all, but no longer will I be your football. I compel you all to make your peace, with the dimming of this candle, warring shall cease.*

* Extinguish and dispose of the candle.

* Put away the bead and refuse to arbitrate or take sides. When matters are settled, make the bead the center of a lovely necklace you wear or give to your partner.

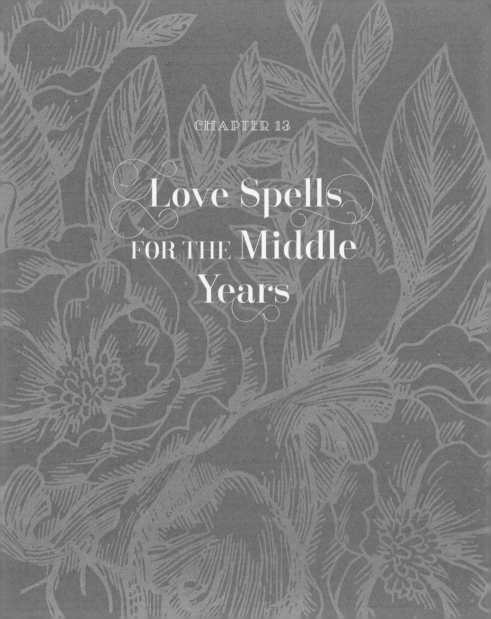

CHAPTER 13

Love Spells
FOR THE Middle Years

The middle years can be the most settled time in a relationship, as we abandon the sometimes unrealistic expectations of perfect love and become relaxed in each other's company. Spells can help to enrich that love and revive romance in mundane periods, when we are focused on paying the bills and fixing the house and don't seem to have time for each other.

We may meet a lifetime partner in our later forties, fifties, or sixties; perhaps a twin soul from our younger days has returned, and all the wisdom and experience we have acquired can make the love work this time around. Spells can help if these middle-year loves are accompanied by a lot of emotional and financial baggage. They are the years when we are anticipating children growing up and leaving home. But, in the modern age, children may stay in the family home into their twenties and even thirties, and those twosome years we anticipated seem to get further away. At the same time, older relatives may need more attention. Stepchildren may cause rifts, and teenage or even adult children can resent a new parent moving in.

Love spells for the middle years, then, focus on finding or reclaiming that twosome out of the debris of Mom and Dad, to reinject romance and revive the old dreams that are sitting on the shelf, gathering dust.

If You Find Your True Love the Second (Or Third) Time Around, but Absolutely Everything and Everyone Seems Allied against You

YOU WILL NEED

Colored sand * A tray * A pointed stick

TIMING

Sunday morning

THE SPELL

* Make a big heap of sand in the center of the tray, saying, *Love will find a way, impossible they say. But though ahead the path looks rough, we can remove every obstacle if we want love enough.*

* Bit by bit, take sand off the top of the heap and smooth it evenly in the tray, saying, *Love will find a way, step by step and stage by stage. For we still have the fire of youth, and the wisdom of middle age.*

* When the heap has almost disappeared, and the sand is smooth, write in the sand, LOVE HAS FOUND A WAY. TOGETHER FOREVER WITH WISDOM AND FIRE, HAPPY SHALL WE STAY.

If You Have Both Waited for the Day the Children Will Leave Home, but They Stay as Adults or Drain Your Finances

YOU WILL NEED

A picture of the whole family when the children were young
* A pile of feathers (use an old down pillow
or buy craftmaking ones)

TIMING

During the waning moon

THE SPELL

* Upstairs, if you have one, smother the picture with feathers, saying,
*Pigtails and lollipops, years in the sun, when you were young, we did
have such fun. But fly away overgrown fledglings, the nest is too small.
We'll love it when you visit or call.*

* Hold the picture at an open window, scattering the feathers to the wind.

* Then scatter any unused feathers out the window as well, saying,
*It's our turn for life, a time for we two, to spread our own wings,
without tripping over or subsidizing you.*

* Make plans.

If Your Partner Has Left You in Middle Age for a New Model

YOU WILL NEED

A pair of old shoes or slippers, preferably your departing
partner's * A new pair of shoes for you

TIMING

Early Saturday evening

THE SPELL

* Hold the old shoes, saying, *You do not do, old worn-out shoes. Cast aside without a glance, Replaced by lust and saccharine romance.*

* Throw them in the garbage.

* Hold your new going-out shoes, saying, *New shoes, new shoes, take me to adventure. Nights of pleasure, days of fun, adored by a gorgeous new lover in the sun.*

* Put on the new shoes, saying, *And if you dare come crawling back, when all has blown up in your face. I'll not be here meekly waiting, but in a brand-new place.*

* Go out wearing your new shoes.

To Go on a Grown-Up Date with Your Partner and Not Talk about the Teenagers or Fixing the Roof

An impossibly expensive fragrance (feed the kids
cheap cereal for a month to pay for it)

Before going out

* Anoint your brow, throat, and heart/inner wrist points with the
  fragrance, saying, *You and me, my love, on an island for two shall we be.*

* Anoint your breasts/chest, womb/just above the genitals, saying,
  *And afterward, you will seduce me. Not in our safe creaky old bed,
  but wherever we are ecstasy led.*

* Enjoy a night when family, home, and work are taboo topics and tell
  the family you will be home late, if at all.

To Avert a Midlife Crisis in Either or Both of You

YOU WILL NEED

Two battery-powered train engines, with hooks
on the back, each pulling a railcar

TIMING

When you know you are drifting apart

THE SPELL

* Wind up or switch on the trains so they run side by side, saying,
  Two trains are we, on separate tracks, pulling other people's carriages.
  No good for our marriage, drifting further away each day.

* Unhook the carriages and join one engine to the other, saying, *Back*
  along the same track, making time for each other. No longer mother/father,
  son or daughter, but each other's lover.

* Make arrangements to offload some responsibilities and go away
  together for a vacation as soon as possible.

If Your Partner Is a Good and Loyal Provider, but Lacking in the Romance Department

YOU WILL NEED

A bag of potatoes * A pack of any meat/meat substitute
that you eat * A bunch of roses * A book of poetry

TIMING

A day or two after the full moon

THE SPELL

* Circle your hands over the potatoes and meat in counterclockwise circles, saying, *Your hard work I/we appreciate, the potatoes and bacon you bring home. But you know it would be good, to add roses with a poem.*

* Add the flowers and the book of poetry and circle your hands clockwise over all four items, saying, *Potatoes and roses, bacon and rhyme, the best combination, so no hesitation, let romance be mine.*

* Cook a meal, including the first two spell ingredients, put the roses in a vase on the table, and read a love poem before serving.

To Renew Your Vows

Note: Do this ritual alone or with a partner.

Grapes, preferably on a long stalk, in a basket
* A new ring for each of you, tied to the
top of the grapes with red thread

TIMING

A significant date

THE SPELL

* Pick a grape, saying, *The vine it binds, your heart to mine, throughout all time.*

* Eat or feed the grape to your partner.

* Pick another grape, saying, *The vine it binds, my life to you. And so we shall be forever true.*

* Continue the spell until you have eaten all the grapes or can eat no more.

* Untie the rings and exchange them, or give yours to your partner later, saying, *Ten years from now, our vows we will once more renew, me and you. Till then no vine we need to bind, we pledge fidelity willingly.*

If You Are in Your Middle Years and Are Still Waiting for the Right Love to Come Along

YOU WILL NEED

A large red candle, surrounded by three smaller
green ones of ascending size in a triangle

TIMING

If you feel like giving up

THE SPELL

* Light the smallest green candle, saying, *Users, losers, stay away. In middle age, I'm past that stage.*

* Light the second-largest green candle, saying, *No control freaks need apply, nor those looking for therapy, Not my idea of ecstasy.*

* Light the largest green candle, saying, *Somewhere out there, must there be, a normal guy/gal, alimony free. Wherever you are, hurry and find me.*

* Light the central red candle from the other three, saying, *For waiting in my ivory tower, I'm far too old. Rescue me now, my knight/princess bold.*

* Blow out all the candles fast and find an entirely new place and activity to try immediately.

If Your Partner Always Forgets Your Birthday

A circle of yellow candles, one for each ten years of your life,
plus one for your coming birthday ✳ An unwritten
romantic birthday card, with the printed message
TO MY DARLING HUSBAND/WIFE, set inside the candle circle

TIMING

Seven days before your birthday

THE SPELL

✳ Circle the date on the calendar and leave the card where s/he
can't miss it.

243

✳ On day 1, light the candles, saying, *Happy birthday to me, this year
feted and adored will I be. Champagne and chocolates, gifts galore,
all I dreamed of and much more.*

✳ Blow out the candles. Continue the spell each night, saying the spell
words faster and louder, and on day 6, as you blow out the candles,
clap loudly.

✳ On day 7, your birthday, light the candles when your partner comes
home, repeating the spell words in your mind.

If Your Children Still Living at Home Oppose Your Efforts to Bring a New Partner into Your Life

YOU WILL NEED

A half-burned candle for you ∗ A new candle for each of the children, enclosing yours ∗ A partly burned candle for your new partner, set away from the group

TIMING

During the crescent moon

THE SPELL

∗ Light your candle and the children's, saying, *Taxi service, meals on wheels, five-star room service, that appeals. You bring home your Shreks, I make them welcome. But it's different story, when your approval I must seek.*

∗ Extinguish their candles, saying, *You dim my light and that's not right. Yet it is me makes you shine bright.*

∗ Replace yours and your partner's candles with new ones, bringing your partner's next to yours.

∗ Light the children's candles farther away, saying, *I always will share with you my light, so accept and respect my new life.*

∗ Leave all the candles burning.

If You Never Seem to be Able to Please Your Partner, No Matter What You Do or Say

YOU WILL NEED

A small flashlight ✳ A dull brown pebble
✳ A clear quartz crystal

TIMING

In darkness, with the curtains drawn

THE SPELL

✳ Shine the flashlight on the brown pebble, saying, *Notice me favorably, you sing the praises of every saint in your life but me. All I do for you, you scarcely see.*

✳ Shine the flashlight on the quartz crystal, saying, *I am your light, I am your spark. I stand by you when days are dark. Day after day I shine for you in vain, your old brown pebble I remain.*

✳ Open the curtains, switch off the flashlight, and go outside. Throw the brown pebble as far away as you can, and have the clear crystal set in a wire finding to wear around your neck.

If Your Partner Has Lost a Lot of Weight or Has Had Cosmetic Surgery and Has Turned into a Stranger

YOU WILL NEED

A budding red rose ✶ A blossoming red rose ✶ A candle ✶ A vase to hold them

TIMING

Sunday

THE SPELL

* Hold your dominant hand over the budding rose, saying, *People turn your head with praise, move on they say from the old days. But whatever others outwardly may see, to me perfect you always will be.*

* Hold your hand over the blossoming rose, repeating the spell words.

* Now light the candle and carefully burn a petal from each rose in the candle flame, saying, *You burn a pathway to my heart. Let not your new image drive us apart.*

* Pluck and mix the petals, including the burned ones, scattering them outdoors, and say, *So the love we had I now reclaim, a rose is a rose by any name.*

If You Are Stuck on a Treadmill
and Never See Each Other

A hamster wheel or ball

During the waning moon

* Roll the wheel across the floor, saying, *Stop the world, stop the wheel. Money comes in, ever faster goes out. The years are whizzing by, of that there's no doubt.*

* Roll it even faster, saying, *Stop the world, stop our life. We pass each other, like ships in the night.*

* Stop the wheel and say, *Life, I ask, send us a way, we can the wheel stop and together stay.*

* Go outdoors and push the wheel down a slope, setting it free, and say, *Set free, shall we also be, to create a life of quality.*

* Brainstorm ways you can downsize or start a joint venture where you can be together much more.

If One of You Is Working Far Away and You Don't Want to Be Apart Anymore

YOU WILL NEED

Two toy boats ∗ Shallow water, such as a stream or the ocean
edge ∗ A bowl of water ∗ A green string ∗ A pond or lake

TIMING

On a full moon day

THE SPELL

∗ Set the two boats sailing in shallow water, but paddle in to retrieve
them, saying, *I wish I may, I wish I might, call you home into my life.*

∗ At home, sail the boats on a bowl of water, saying, *I call you home,
we will find a way. I would not be parted from you another day.*

∗ The next morning, tie the boats together with nine knots, saying, *I call
you home into my life. I wish I may, I wish I might, have you daily within
my sight.*

∗ Give the two joined boats to a child.

If You Live Together, But Warring Sets of Teenage or Adult Children Are Making Your Life Hell

YOU WILL NEED

Modeling clay ✶ A radio ✶ A sealable bag

TIMING

Whenever the situation becomes unbearable

THE SPELL

✶ Make a figure out of modeling clay for each of the warring children. Name each one, and say, *Let these battles instantly cease. Act like grown-ups, live in peace.*

✶ Put the figures in a circle around the radio, turning it up to full volume, then gradually lowering it to silence, and say, *Silent be, unless you can act civilized in our company.*

✶ Roll the figures back into a ball, place the ball in the bag, and seal it, saying, *One family, joined by your father/mother and me. Learn some manners, put away the daggers, so we can all sit around one table, using metal cutlery.*

✶ Bury the closed bag, saying, *Bury the hatchet and not in me. Learn to act decently, then dug up you can be.*

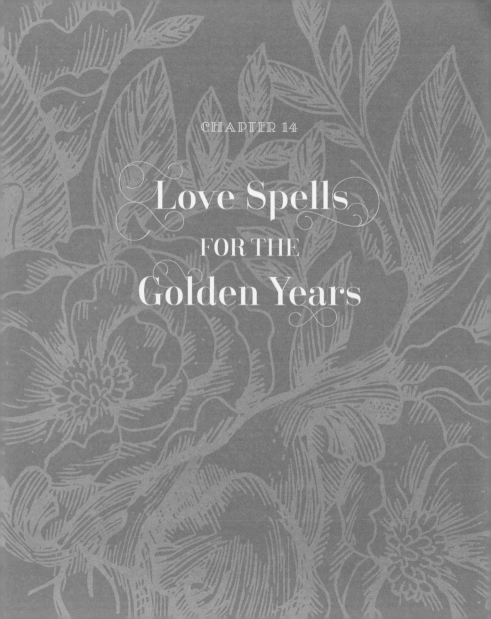

CHAPTER 14

Love Spells
FOR THE
Golden Years

he later sixties and beyond are now times not for the rocking chair and weekly activities clubs, but of exploration, discovering new interests, and often continuing working. We may find ourselves expected to provide child care, help pay for college, or make down payments for houses for our grandchildren and great-grandchildren at a time when we want the money to enjoy life. If we're still working, we might want to reduce our hours and, when we're retired, develop creative and spiritual interests, live in the place of our dreams, and travel. But sometimes our partner doesn't share our dreams.

Issues such as anger and excess alcohol consumption, manageable when a couple was working, suddenly flare up. If one person is a workaholic, and won't hand over the reins of a business, the other can become frustrated waiting for the adventure time that moves further away. As I am now in this age group myself, I have witnessed a huge upsurge of clients from sixty through their nineties who want good love and so I have created over the last twenty years love spells specifically for the golden years. All the spells in this chapter represent real-life love dilemmas I have been asked to help resolve.

If You Are Caring Full Time for Grandchildren and Great-Grandchildren and Are Deprived of Time for Your Partner

YOU WILL NEED

Two long sticks to make a crossroads outdoors
* A toy donkey * Two clear crystals * Small
stones piled in the center of the crossroads

TIMING

During the waxing moon

THE SPELL

* Stand at your homemade crossroads, holding the donkey, and say, *Beast of burden, you struggle with your load. To new generations you offer your care, but time for you and* [name partner] *is never there.*

* Put the donkey down and bury the crystals in the stones, saying, *Beast of burden, too heavy the load. Make time for each other, not just as father and mother.*

* Uncover the crystals, leaving them in the light, and say, *Old donkey, you are free, to gallop not stagger, where you most would like to be.*

* Give the donkey to one of your grandchildren and rearrange your schedule.

If You Are Married to Dr. Jekyll and Mr./ Ms. Hyde and No One Will Believe You

YOU WILL NEED

A larger paper figure, one side white with a halo, the other
side red with huge teeth, attached to a popsicle stick
* A smaller blank paper figure, representing you
* A small metal chain wrapped around both figures

TIMING

In sunlight

THE SPELL

* Turn the larger figure around, saying, *Angel or demon, Jekyll and Hyde, when others meet you, they see your good side. I suffer in silence, no one will believe, your viciousness I know I must leave.*

* Unwrap the chain so the figures separate.

* Let your partner's figure drop to the floor, repeating the spell words.

* Color your figure in rainbow shades, throw away the other figure, and say, *Dr. Jekyll and Mr./Ms. Hyde, still you will your dark side hide, till a new victim you do find. But I leave you far behind.*

To Enjoy the Golden Years
Traveling with Your Partner

YOU WILL NEED

Two miniature silver globe charms on a
necklace * A globe of the world

TIMING

On retirement

THE SPELL

* Put on the necklace with your charms.

* Stand in the center of your home, touch your charms, and then spin
  your globe, saying, *Opening every possibility, take us where happiness
  and fulfillment we shall see.*

* Touch the charms, then, holding the globe in one hand, spin it,
  standing just inside the front door, and say, *Adventure we can, adventure
  we will, not wait for tomorrow, with maybe and might. Today life begins,
  filled with delight.*

* Open the door and step through it, touch the charms, then spin the
  globe, and say, *The path to life calls, let us with joy experience it all.*

* Before traveling, touch the charms and spin the globe.

* Wear one globe charm at a time and make wishes on them
  whenever needed.

To Find a New Partner Later in Life

YOU WILL NEED

A gold candle ∗ A mirror ∗ A yellow rosebud,
symbol of love in the golden years ∗ A vase

TIMING

At sunset

THE SPELL

∗ Light the candle and, gazing in the mirror, hold the rose, and say,
  *Never too old, in my days of pure gold. Come love's bright dance, bring me
  this night late-blooming romance.*

∗ Still holding the rose, say, *In this flame, entrance me, excite me, delight
  me. Let me see whom you may be.*

∗ Blow out the candle, blink, and in the afterglow you may see in the
  mirror or your mind a glimpse of the right person and where you may
  meet him/her.

∗ Place the flower in the vase, repeating the spell nightly until the rose
  fades. Each night you may see the person more clearly. It may be
  someone you already know.

If Your Aging Partner Runs Off with the Savings with a New Partner Young Enough to Be Your Grandchild

YOU WILL NEED

An empty pot * Pins * A map showing where
your ex-partner is living * A magnet

TIMING

As soon as you realize that your ex-partner has run off

THE SPELL

* Shake the empty pot, saying, *You stole away like a thief in the night, taking what was not yours by right. Yet I do not ill-wish you, hex nor curse. Your bed you've made, for better or worse.*

* Scatter the pins over the map and pass the magnet over it, collecting them one by one and dropping them into the pot, and say, *Return only what is mine, your flawed love can yours keep. I remind your mind, awake or asleep, repay me instantly, and then you can live unhappily.*

* Each day shake the pot, repeating the second set of spell words.

If Your Partner Is Flirting While S/he Is Not with You

YOU WILL NEED

A child's drum, with your partner's name
written on it in nonporous ink * Drumsticks

TIMING

When you know your partner will be flirting

THE SPELL

* Play the drum gently and rhythmically with the drumsticks, increasing the speed and intensity as you say, faster and faster, *Boys and girls come out to play, but not maybe at seventy* [use your partner's age]. *Bit of a cougar/super stud too, when your rheumatism's not plaguing you.*

* Bang more slowly, saying more and more slowly, *Chasing the youngsters if they slow down, You think you're the coolest guy/chick in town. But hey you can't push back the clock. I tell you now this must stop.*

* At that point, stop drumming, and cross and squeeze the drumsticks together.

If You and Your Partner Want to Start an Amazing Creative Business in a New Part of the Country Or the World Upon Retirement

A sensible hat * A fun hat * Bubbles and a bubble wand

TIMING

Wednesday

THE SPELL

* Before going outdoors to blow bubbles, put on your sensible hat and take it off, saying, *Retired but inspired, sorry Mr./Ms. Sensible, you'll have to wait a decade or two, before I'm ready for you.*

* Put on your fun hat, go outdoors, and start blowing bubbles.

* Name your wish for your new venture and then blow a bubble, saying, *Wishes are made to come true, and so I send this wish in the sky. So it will be fulfilled before* [name time line for fulfillment] *comes by.*

* Keep blowing the bubbles and making wishes for the new venture until all the bubbles or wishes are done.

* Give your sensible hat to charity and wear your fun hat as you embark on your new life.

If You Need to Say Goodbye to a Partner with Dementia for Whom You Can No Longer Care

YOU WILL NEED

A white candle ★ Your wedding photo and a selection of photos of you all and the family through the years

TIMING

Alone, the night before you part

THE SPELL

* Light the candle and breathe softly in the flame, saying, *Till death us do part we vowed and how I have tried. But to the person I married I must say good-bye.*

* Look at the photos by candlelight, saying, *These are our memories that will never die, golden moments rushing by. But the love between us will stay in my heart, though now cruel circumstance forces us to part.*

* Blow out the candle, sending love to the person your partner was, is, and will become.

* Make the pictures into a memory board for your partner's new room.

If Your New Partner Won't Have Anything to Do with Your Family and Excludes You From His/Hers

YOU WILL NEED

A patchouli incense stick ✳ Two overlapping circles drawn on white paper ✳ A red jasper for your partner and one for each member of his family ✳ Pink crystals for you and each member of your family

TIMING

During the crescent moon

THE SPELL

* Light the incense stick and draw a line in smoke down the middle of the circle overlap, saying, *These divisions need not be. No walls of stone do I see.*

* Put a crystal for you and one for your partner in the center of the overlapping circles, saying, *Love we share and love to spare, my family can be yours and yours be mine. We do not need a dividing line.*

* Shake all the remaining crystals together in your cupped hands, saying, *One family, united with love through you and me.*

* Toss the family crystals into the overlapping circles and blow out the candle.

* Set up a joint get-together.

If You Have Met a New Love and Your Family Says S/He Is Only after Your Money

YOU WILL NEED

Pruning shears or strong scissors * Two yellow
roses with thorns * A pink rose

TIMING

Monday

THE SPELL

* With pruning shears, cut the thorns off the yellow roses, saying,
  I see petals, you see thorns. You see deception, but s/he is the one.

* Discard the thorns, saying, *Love later in life is just as sweet, so my
  new love you shall meet. No thorns, no barbs, but with open hearts.*

* Add a pink rose with thorns removed, for each objecting
  family member.

* Invite the family, placing the thornless roses as the centerpiece on
  the table. Give each family member a rose to take home and keep your
  two roses until they fade.

If You Both Want to Downsize and Travel, but Your Family Wants You to Leave the Family Home as a Bequest

YOU WILL NEED

A blue candle

Two pictures of your home, printed on paper
suitable to make paper boats ✻ Two paper boats
(GO TO HTTPS://WWW.WIKIHOW.COM/MAKE-A-PAPER-BOAT)

TIMING

The beginning of a month

THE SPELL:

✻ Light the candle and set the pictures of the home, one on top of the other, so candlelight shines on them, saying, *Weekly lunches, Sunday tea, not the future for your Dad/Mom and me. We love you dearly, but our time has come to up and run.*

✻ Make the pictures into paper boats, repeating the spell words, and blow out the candle.

✻ Go sail your paper boats in the bath, on a pond, a river, or the open sea.

If Your Family Is Pressuring You to Pay for the Grandchildren's College Tuition, Which Will Compromise You and Your Partner's Plans

YOU WILL NEED

A spoon ∗ A sealed jar of flour or rice
∗ A kitchen scale with balancing pans

TIMING

Before a family conference

THE SPELL

∗ Start spooning the flour/rice into each pan alternately, but put double in the second one, saying, *One for me, two for you. Soon our resources will be run through.*

∗ As the one pan starts to tip, start spooning some of the mix into the lighter pan, saying, *One for you, one for me. Seems much fairer, don't you see?*

∗ When the pans are balanced, close the jar, saying, *But this we keep in reserve, robbing ourselves won't our future serve. We worked hard, you do the same. We're not a bottomless jar. Time to follow our own star.*

∗ Use what is in the scale pans to add to the family meal and make suggestions as to how the younger generation can subsidize themselves.

If You Have Lost Your Partner and Everyone Is Trying to Rush You to Move On

A candle whose fragrance reminds you of your partner
* Photos and a few treasures belonging to your partner
* A white candle * Fresh flowers, photos,
or treasures, for memory table

TIMING

An evening alone

THE SPELL

265

* Light the candle and say, *Till death us do part, we vowed. But then so unfairly it came. One day life may be good again, but never will be the same.*

* Blow gently in the candle, saying, *In my own time I will let you go. But death does not part, you live forever in my heart.*

* Leave the candle burning while you look at the photos.

* Create a memory table with photos, treasures, a white candle, and fresh flowers, the kind your partner loved, moving on with your life, step by step, how, when, and if you are ready, whether it takes months, years, or forever.

If You Have to Say Goodbye to a Secret Love Whose Funeral You Could Not Attend

YOU WILL NEED

A flat dark stone for every month/year you were together
∗ A packet of his/her favorite flower or herb seeds ∗ A ring
s/he gave you or, if not, one you have bought yourself

TIMING

Until you have used all the stones

THE SPELL

∗ Go to a secluded place where you used to meet.

∗ On the first day, place a stone, planting a few seeds around it and
watering the seeds. Say, *This cairn is memorial to what we shared,
though I could not be at your passing, my soul was there. I wear your ring
until together we can be, though none my broken heart may see.*

∗ Wear the ring around your neck on a chain.

∗ Continue adding stones, one on top of the other, until they and
the seeds are all in place.

If Your Partner Has a Serious Drinking or Gambling Problem That Has Become Worse in Retirement

YOU WILL NEED

Gambling chips, betting slips, or a miniature bottle of spirits   *   Garden bone meal or a few cooked chicken bones, crushed in soil   *   Two twigs stripped of leaves

TIMING

The end of the moon cycle

THE SPELL

* Go where there is bare earth, on the route your partner walks/drives to gamble/buy alcohol.

* Dig a hole and in it drop the gambling chips or pour out the alcohol, saying, *Dust to dust, may this destruction die, draining our savings, making you lie. Drinking/gambling I bid you good-bye.*

* Add the bone meal and fill in the hole, marking the spot with crossed sticks, and say, *The last drink/gamble buried here shall be. Do not cross this line or lose everything—including me.*

If Your Partner Won't Slow Down at Work and You Want to Travel and Have Fun Together

A helium balloon tethered outdoors with a string to a
large brick or stone ✳ Luggage labels ✳ A blue pen

TIMING

When s/he is too busy to go on a trip

THE SPELL

* Shake the string attached to the balloon, but don't let the balloon go, saying, *When you're a hundred and five, to life you'll maybe come alive. You've tied a millstone round your neck, slaving harder more and more. But these are the years we've been waiting for.*

* On the luggage labels, write dreams you've talked about fulfilling and attach them to the string.

* Release the balloon and let it fly away, saying, *Free you shall be, come with me. Don't wait till a hundred and five, till you finally come alive.*

If Your Partner Spends His/Her Retirement Watching Television and Won't Go Anywhere or Do Anything

YOU WILL NEED

The television remote control

TIMING

When your partner is not in the room

THE SPELL

* Put the remote on a flat surface, remove the batteries, and pass both hands counterclockwise over it to disenchant it, saying, *From life retired, much too tired. Watching the world on a TV screen, cheering people we don't know, on every boring reality show, I really want to scream.*

* Replace the batteries with used ones, saying, *I separate you from your lifeline, to join real life it's truly time.*

* Hide all new batteries and suggest that you go out together to buy new ones, stop for lunch, and visit a travel agent.

* Do this weekly until s/he gets the idea.

If Your Partner Is Stingy with Money and Won't Let You Spend Anything

A bag of mothballs ★ One or two printouts of
your bank statements ★ A container

TIMING

When your partner says you can't afford something and you know you can

THE SPELL

* Open the bag of mothballs, shred the papers, and put them in the bag of mothballs, resealing the bag in a container, and say, *Moths in your wallet/ purse, chomping away, at the happiness we could share every day.*

* Bury the bag in a marked spot for 48 hours, dig it up, pour out the mothballs and shredded paper in the center of the table, and say, *Moths, moths fly away, don't come back any day. What are we saving for, till we're a hundred and four? No way.*

* Vacuum or sweep up the shredded paper and mothballs and make a purchase.

* Repeat when necessary.

If One of You Becomes Seriously Ill or Disabled

271

YOU WILL NEED

Dried lavender ✳ A picture of you and your partner when you first met and a recent one, secured face-to-face with green ribbon ✳ Dried sage ✳ Dried thyme ✳ Dried rosemary ✳ A green drawstring bag or purse

TIMING

Friday

THE SPELL

✳ Scatter a circle of dried lavender counterclockwise around the pictures, saying, *In sickness and in health, that was our vow. And that promise is and will remain, as strong as it is now.*

✳ Scatter a clockwise circle of sage around the lavender, repeating the spell words.

✳ Scatter a circle of thyme counterclockwise around the sage and a circle of rosemary clockwise around the thyme.

✳ Scoop the herbs into the bag, keeping it with the tied pictures.

✳ Touch it when things get hard, saying, *Lavender, sage, rosemary, thyme, for good or ill, hardship or wealth, I will love you forever as yourself.*

If You Know Your Partner Will Never Change, But You Want or Need to Stay

A small, sealed pack of modeling clay
★ Salt ★ Orange ribbons

TIMING

Saturday

THE SPELL

* Hold the sealed pack of clay, saying, *I dreamed someday my prince/ss would come, but s/he sure got lost on the way. I am too old to start again, so together we must stay.*

* Unwrap the clay and make two figures side by side, saying, *I will make my life, my own way. Too old to go, that I know, but coexisting peacefully, and sharing a home amicably.*

* Sprinkle salt on each figure and hang them with orange ribbons from adjoining branches on the same tree or bush.

* Hang ribbons weekly from the tree until the figures crumble.

If Your Partner Is Your Best Friend, But Not Your Lover

YOU WILL NEED

Two paper dolls colored red ✳ Red ribbon ✳ A fire pit
or a fireproof container ✳ Scarlet flower petals

TIMING

Tuesday

THE SPELL

* Hold the dolls in your open, cupped hands, saying, *We used to make love under the stars, the blanket on the ground. So how with the passing of the years can passion no longer be found? We're not too old, so let's be bold.*

* Tie the paper dolls together with red ribbon, saying, *Three times the lover's knot secure, passion I call you and romance. Once more be bound in love's ecstatic dance.*

* After three days, release the figures, saying, *Three times the lover's knot flies free, may passion return with intensity. Like this all-consuming flame, I call fierce lust, in love's own name.*

* Throw the figures on an outdoor fire or burn them in a fireproof container, adding scarlet petals.

* Go away for a wild weekend.

CHAPTER 15

Love Charms, Amulets, AND Talisman Spells

Making love charms dates back to ancient Egyptian times. Today, lovers wear matching pendants, each with half a silver heart. Identical crystals, especially jade or rose quartz, the crystals of lasting faithful love, are also frequently empowered and either kept together in a small bag or purse or one each carried by lovers when apart.

There are many forms of love charms—bags of empowered herbs and dried flowers, each with a love meaning, love knots entwined with yours and a lover's hair, or small dolls tied with ribbon and used to bolster commitment. The spell actions and words charge a love charm, according to the intention of the spell, with the power to call and keep love and protect your relationship.

There are three different kinds of "love charms." Love amulets will store protection that can be called on at any time over months or used in the background; for example, a fidelity herb bag hung over the marital bed. Love charms are small objects or bags of crystals or herbs over which magical spells have been chanted or on which magick words are engraved or painted. They have no limits to their life as long as they remain intact and any visible markings do not fade. A charm increases in power as it is used to attract love or increase commitment. A love talisman is a charm made and/or empowered for a single specific purpose.

A Charm to Bring Love into Your Life

YOU WILL NEED

A small item that is precious to you
* Two matching jade charms or crystals
* A green scarf * A green purse or bag

TIMING

Seven days

THE SPELL

* On day 1, hold the precious item, saying, *This holds my heart, my happiness. I give its power to bring the love who will mean no less.*

* Knot the item with the jade charms in the scarf until day 7.

* On day 7 unwrap the scarf. Hold the beloved item in your dominant hand and the jade in the other, saying, *I transfer the power, at this hour. Bring me the love who a thousand times more precious will be, than this that means so much to me.*

* Keep your love charms in the bag or purse when you go out socially or on an online date.

A Nineteenth-Century Love Talisman
to Make Your Lover More Romantic
or to Attract a Romantic Lover

YOU WILL NEED

A beeswax candle * An old-fashioned fountain pen
and black ink * A small square of white paper
* A fabric purse

TIMING

The first Friday on or after the full moon

THE SPELL

* Light the candle.

* Using the fountain pen and black ink, write as small as possible on the paper, *I, [your name], command in the name of Aphrodite and Venus, Goddesses of love, for my love to come to me romantically with tenderness, gentleness, and infinite adoration, and stay with me eternally. Lady Aphrodite, Venus of desire, I call him/her now in this candle fire.*

* Fold the paper as small as possible and seal it with three drops of beeswax from the candle.

* When the wax is set, put the love charm in the purse and keep it next to your bed.

A Talisman to Make Someone You Like a Lot Ask You to Be His/Her Date for a Major Event

A beeswax candle on a heatproof tray ✻ A sharp
knife ✻ Dried rosemary ✻ A piece of silk

TIMING

As soon as you know about the event

THE SPELL

Light the candle, saying six times, *Invite me* [Name], *delight me.*

✻ As the candle melts, say six times, *As this wax melts, so may his/her heart be molten to me. Invite me, delight me. So shall it be.*

✻ Using a knife, in the cooling wax around the candle, draw a heart with your entwined initials. Sprinkle rosemary all around, saying, *Rosemary for remembrance, remember me, notice me, invite me. So shall it be.*

✻ Cut around the heart and the rosemary, wrap the talisman in silk, open it before bed each night, and repeat, *Invite me, delight me. So shall it be.*

A Viking Love Amulet to Survive Difficult Times

YOU WILL NEED

A letter opener ✳ Two red candles, side by side
✳ A red permanent marker pen or red paint and a
paintbrush ✳ A round white stone ✳ A red bag

TIMING

Friday after sunset

THE SPELL

* With a letter opener, etch on each candle the Gebo rune
  for love (see drawing) that survives every difficulty.

* Light the first candle, saying, *I release the power of the rune
  into our lives, that we shall together survive.*

* Light the second candle, repeating the spell words.

* Hold both lighted candles, one in each hand, joining the flames
  momentarily, and say, *So shall two remain one through hardship,
  till time is run.*

* By the light of the candles, draw in red the Gebo rune on the stone,
  repeating the second set of spell words.

* Leave the candle to burn through.

* Keep the stone in the bag and hold it to call its powers
  when your love is tested.

An Ancient Egyptian Talisman
to Call Back Lost Love

YOU WILL NEED

A circle of modeling clay * A small etching
tool or a sharp knife

TIMING

Friday

THE SPELL

* On the clay, etch the Tyet, or Buckle of Isis, the supreme
  goddess (see drawing).

* As you do this, say, *The blood of Isis and the power of Isis and the words
  of Isis, who called back her lost love Osiris that they might make sweet love
  once more, bring my lost love back to my door.*

* When the clay is dry, trace over the image with the index finger of your
  dominant hand, saying, *The power of Isis and the words of Isis and the
  blood of Isis, you who brought fertility to the parched land, bring new life
  to this lost love that s/he will once more in love take my hand.*

* Cast your talisman in running water.

An Ancient Egyptian Daughters of Hathor Commitment Ritual

YOU WILL NEED

A red candle ★ Seven red ribbons, one for each
daughter of the Goddess Hathor (see drawing),
who all rule committed love and fidelity

TIMING

The hour before sunset

THE SPELL

* Light the candle, setting the ribbons one in
  front of the other, next to it.

* Knot ribbons 1 and 2 together, saying,
  Daughters of Hathor, our love is true.
  I ask that we may forever together stay.
  Mother Hathor, guide our way.

* Continue, repeating the spell words as a continuous chant,
  knotting ribbon 2 to 3, 3 to 4, 4 to 5, 5 to 6, 6 to 7, and 7 to 1.

* As you complete the ribbon circle, say, *May the circle of our love*
  never be broken, may passion and devotion be always in our hearts,
  never to part.

* Let the candle burn through. Hang the circle of ribbons
  over your bed.

A Twin Charm Ritual for a Long-Term Relationship Where You Are Often Apart

YOU WILL NEED

Two small garments, the more intimate the better,
one from each of you * A silver or gold charm that is
divided in two, each half on a separate neck chain

TIMING

During the crescent moon

THE SPELL

* Wash the two garments in warm water and let them air-dry.

* Wrap the charm halves in the dried garments for 24 hours, saying,
  When we are apart, this charm joins me to your heart.

* Then hold the two halves of the charm together in your open, cupped
  hands, saying, *Together forever though we may be far away, my love will
  with you constantly stay. Touch your charm and you will know, with you my
  heart will always go.*

* Wear your half of the charm and give or send the other half to your love.

A Gold Fidelity Amulet for a Wedding or an Anniversary

A pair of gold earrings or a small green and
pink unakite, the twin soul crystal on a chain or in a wire
finding ✻ A small green drawstring bag, containing
dried rosemary or yarrow and salt ✻ Frankincense and
myrrh incense sticks, crossed in a double holder

TIMING

After the wedding or an anniversary

284

THE SPELL

* Attach the earrings or crystal to the drawstring of the bag, saying,
  *Love, I pledge my love to you, ever faithful ever true. You are my love
  and ever will be, until there is no salt left in the sea.*

* Light the two incense sticks.

* Pass the bag with the attached gold or crystal through the smoke,
  repeating the spell words.

* Leave the incense to burn through, and hang the bag over your bed.

* Replace the herbs when they lose their fragrance.

A Love Pomander Amulet for
Your First Home Together

YOU WILL NEED

An orange ✳ A skewer ✳ Whole cloves ✳ Two tablespoons
of ground cinnamon, two tablespoons of ground coriander,
and 1 tablespoon of ground orris, mixed in
a dish ✳ A green or red ribbon

TIMING

When you move in together

THE SPELL

✳ Pierce the orange skin with the skewer to create small holes, not cutting
through to the flesh.

✳ Push the cloves into the orange, forming unbroken rings of cloves,
so the entire orange is covered, making a wish for each clove for your
future happiness together.

✳ Gently roll the completed pomander in the dish containing the spice
mix, saying as a soft chant, *This is our sanctuary. Happy within it always
may we be.*

✳ Shake off any residual powder and tie the pomander with green or
red ribbon.

✳ Hang the pomander in a warm, dry place.

A Traditional Love Wish Talisman to Call Love within Three Moons

YOU WILL NEED

A silver heart or a heart-shaped rose quartz crystal ✳ White petals in a basket

TIMING

During the crescent moon or soon after

THE SPELL

* Stand where you can see the moon, holding your love talisman.

* Turn it over three times, repeating each time you do so, *One for love, you moon above, send love to me. Two for love, you moon above, fidelity. Three for love, you moon above, love eternally. May s/he come soon, within three moons.*

* Put the talisman in the basket of flower petals and, holding it to the moon, repeat the spell words.

* Leave the talisman in the basket all night on an indoor window ledge, and in the morning remove the talisman, scattering the petals in a crescent-moon shape outdoors.

* Wear the talisman or keep it in a pouch under your pillow.

A Love Charm Bag to Increase the Love and Passion of Someone You Love

Nine hairs from your hairbrush, attached to a green thread
* A tiny cut-out red-paper or red-velvet heart * A pinch of
dried mint, a pinch of parsley, a pinch of basil, and a few dried
bay leaves * A silver or copper neck chain * A small pink
drawstring bag * A white candle * A silver or gold hand bell

TIMING

10 P.M. Friday

THE SPELL

* One by one, add everything to the bag, except the candle and the bell.

* Light the candle, ringing the bell ten times, and say, *I charm you*
  [Name], *enchant, bedazzle, bewitch and enrapture, your loving heart
  I would capture. Within this bag, my magick calls, you cannot resist me
  at all.*

* Blow out the candle, saying, *Night and darkness speak his/her name,
  silently I do the same.*

* Call your love silently. Wear or carry the spell bag.

An Iron Love Amulet to Protect Your Relationship from Jealousy and Malice

YOU WILL NEED

Water in which new iron or steel nails have been
soaked in a metal bowl for 24 hours, known magically as warrior
water * Dried dill or rosemary * A hematite or polished
iron pyrite crystal * A picture of you and your partner

TIMING

Tuesday

THE SPELL

* After 24 hours of soaking the nails, add the dill or rosemary to
  the warrior water, saying, *By the power of iron and the power of dill,
  I protect our love from all ill will.*

* Take out the nails and bury them near your front door, scattering drops
  of the warrior water in circles around and over the crystal, and say,
  Warrior water and power of Mars, stand protector for this love of ours.

* Keep the crystal with a picture of you and your partner.

Another Ancient Egyptian Isis Charm to Call Twin Soul Love

YOU WILL NEED

A thin waterproof red marker pen or a small paintbrush and red paint ✴ A long thin piece of paper ✴ Wind chimes or a string of bells ✴ Red thread

TIMING

During the full moon

ANKH

THE SPELL

✴ With the red marker pen, cover both sides of the paper with the Ankh symbol, shown above, the Egyptian lasting love hieroglyph of Osiris and Isis, the divine couple, saying, *Twin soul come find me, through the deserts of time. That our Ankh love will shine, like the sun shimmering perpetually.*

✴ Ring the chimes softly and continuously and say, *I call, I wait, no other will do. Twin Soul, it shall, it can only be you.*

✴ Attach the strip of paper with the thread to the wind chimes or bells and hang them where the wind will catch them, repeating the second set of spell words.

A Three-Metal Love Charm If Love Is Slow to Appear in Your Life

YOU WILL NEED

A gold earring ✷ A blue bag or purse ✷ A silver ring
✷ A copper ring ✷ Dried rose petals or lavender heads

TIMING

10 P.M. Friday

THE SPELL

* Put the gold earring in the bag, saying, *Gold of the sun for love everlasting, true love to me swiftly bring.*

* Place the silver ring in the bag, saying, *Silver of the moon, for love's own call, send the right love who will offer me all.*

* Place the copper ring in the bag, saying, *Copper of Venus, passion send, my Twin Soul and love without end.*

* Add the flowers, saying, *Gold, silver, copper, wrapped in flowers of gentleness, I ask for life soon, no more no less.*

* Take the bag outdoors, shake it six times, scatter the flowers, and wear all three metal items when you go on a date or engage in online dating.

A Locket Amulet for a Secret Love

A musk incense cone ✻ A small picture of your love
✻ A locket ✻ A picture of a family member
✻ White roses, the symbol of secrecy

TIMING

At the new moon

THE SPELL

✳ Light the incense, putting the picture of your love in the locket and the family picture on top.

✳ Close the locket and pass it nine times through the incense smoke, saying, *Not to be spoken, never seen, but next to my heart, my true love always will be.*

✳ Pluck the rose petals and scatter half the petals counterclockwise around the locket, repeating the spell words.

✳ When the incense is burned through, mix it with the remaining petals. Release this mixture outdoors, saying, *Love fly free, to wherever my true love may be. I wear this amulet close to my heart, and so we never shall be apart.*

A Ring-Binding Charm If You Want to Get Married But Your Partner Doesn't

YOU WILL NEED

Six green candles, set around a ring ★ A ring borrowed
from a happily married person (not a wedding ring)

TIMING

During the full moon

THE SPELL

* Light the candles clockwise, reading the following words taken from the Song of Solomon (8:6–7): *Set me as a seal upon thine heart, as a seal upon thine arm, for love is as strong as death. Many waters cannot quench love, neither can floods drown it. If a man would give all the substance of his house for love, he would be contented.*

* When the candles are burned through, sleep with the ring on your wedding finger (or any finger on which it will fit).

* In the morning, return the ring to its owner.

* Put a copy of the verse, folded small, above the lintel of your front door.

A Relationship Dedication Rite
When You Can't Legally Marry

YOU WILL NEED

A green candle ∗ A ring given to you by your
partner ∗ A small waterproof bag ∗ A basil plant

TIMING

On a moonlit Monday night

THE SPELL

∗ Light the candle and touch the ring, saying, *Round and round the ring of truth, Love in age and love in youth. Love in sickness and in health, love in death and love in wealth.*

∗ Place the ring in the bag and bury the bag in the soil surrounding the basil plant, saying, *Basil of fidelity, I pledge my love to you eternally, and receive the love you daily give to me.*

∗ Blow out the candle. Sit in the moonlight, saying, *Be with me through dark and light, stay with me by day and night, you who are precious in my sight.*

∗ After 24 hours, dig up the ring and restore it to your finger. Do the same if your partner has a ring.

A Ribbon Charm to Increase Commitment with Your Chosen Love

Seven red ribbons ✶ Two small dolls,
such as worry dolls

TIMING

Starting on a Monday night

THE SPELL

* Tie the seven ribbons together at one end.

* Tie three knots around the dolls with the ribbons, naming a doll for each of you, and say, *Three times the lover's knot secures, firm be the knots, long may the love endure.*

* Keep the knotted dolls under your pillow for three nights.

* On the fourth morning, take the dolls outside and undo the knots one by one, shaking each cord in the air, and say, *Three times the lover's knot flies free. The love is now bound between him/her and me, willingly and eternally.*

* Retie the dolls, loosely this time, with the seven ribbons.

* Suspend them hidden in a bush or tree in or near your intended's home or his/her workplace if you work together.

A Second Knot Binding Charm If You Want Your Love to Move in with You

YOU WILL NEED

An undergarment from each of you * A long red ribbon

TIMING

Starting on a Thursday morning

THE SPELL

* Tie the two garments together with the ribbon in three knots, saying, *I love you by day, I love you by night. We share lovely lovemaking, and then you take flight. I wind, I bind, these knots secure. Live with me, with me stay. Don't at 3 A.M. always slip away.*

* Hide the knotted undergarments for three nights.

* On the fourth morning, go outside and free the knots, saying, *Three times the lover's knot flies free. Live with me, stay with me. So must it be.*

* Put the undergarments side by side on the bed. Cut a length of the ribbon, retie it in three knots, and attach it to something you wear next to your heart.

A Star Love Charm for Meeting
the Partner of Your Dreams

YOU WILL NEED

A silver star charm, star brooch, or clip

TIMING

As the stars are appearing

THE SPELL

* Focus on the brightest star or Venus, if visible.

* Hold the charm upward to the stars, saying three times, *Star light, star bright, most dazzling star I see tonight. I wish I may, I wish I might, find the love who for me is right.*

* Press the charm close to your heart, then to your lips, and up to the stars, saying, *Star light, star bright, most dazzling star I see tonight. I wish I may, I wish I might, find my love to share lasting delight.*

* If you know the person, whisper his/her name into your charm.

* Carry or wear your charm, for you can find love in the most unexpected places.

A Magnetic Charm Bag to Draw
You to Your Twin Soul

YOU WILL NEED

Two bar magnets * A green purse or drawstring
bag * Cloves * Matching jade crystals

TIMING

Wednesday, during the waxing moon

THE SPELL

* Holding a magnet in each hand, say, *Attract to me my twin soul love, that
  I will magnetically be drawn to him/her and s/he to me, and know instantly,
  this is the love meant to be.*

* Let the magnets join, repeating the spell words, and put them in
  the bag.

* Add a few cloves to the bag, saying, *Cloves of fire, pierce my new love with
  unquenchable desire.*

* Put in the jade crystals, saying, *Jade, bring fidelity, that long and joyful
  shall our union be.*

* Before going out socially, or logging onto social media or a dating site,
  shake the bag nine times, saying, *As magnets may we drawn together be,
  Twin Soul I attract you now to me.*

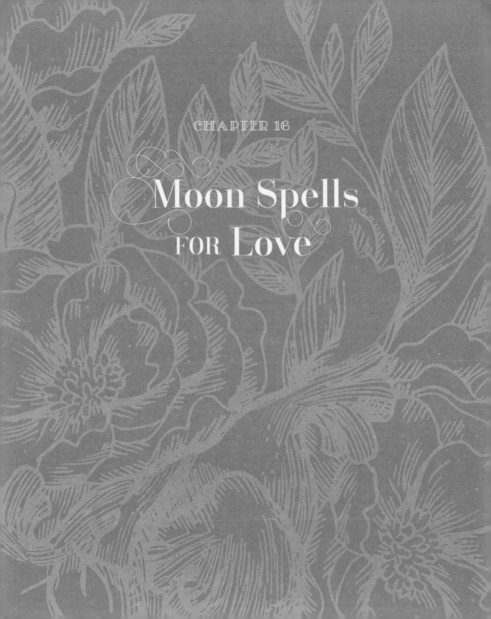

CHAPTER 16

Moon Spells
FOR Love

F rom ancient times, the moon, especially the full moon, has been associated with love and fertility. Moon spells are enhanced by the power of the moon in each of its four stages. The waxing phase begins when the crescent moon is first seen in the sky on day 3 or 4 of the cycle, until the night of the full moon.

The crescent moon is powerful for new beginnings in love, and the waxing moon for romance and increasing commitment in relationships and reconciliation. The full moon is good for consummating love/conceiving a child, sex magick, and making a permanent love commitment. The waning or old moon follows the full moon and lasts until the waning crescent can no longer be seen in the sky. It removes obstacles to love and lessens the influence of negative people.

The moon passes through the dark of the moon, or the new moon, during the intervening three days after the waning moon and before the crescent appears and is not visible in the sky. The dark of the moon is good for sacred sex and for love not sanctioned by family or community.

The current moon phase can be found by looking online (https://www.moongiant.com/). The weather or astrology section of a daily newspaper generally mentions the moon phase and days of the lunar cycle, and there are some excellent moon calendars offering this essential information.

A Crescent Moon Love Wish

A silver candle, silver being the color of the moon
★ A strip of purple paper and a silver pen ★ A pot of soil

TIMING

On crescent moon night, even if cloudy

THE SPELL

* Light the candle.

* By its light, write your love wish but tell no one.

* Hold one end of the paper close to the flame and, when it starts burning, drop it in the soil, saying, *Maiden Moon, as you do grow, I release my wish, asking you make it so. And when next month I see your crescent shine, I will know the wish is mine.*

* Blow out the candle and bury the wish in the soil while facing the crescent moon outdoors.

A Crescent to Full Moon Ritual If You Are Getting Discouraged with Fertility Tests and Treatment

YOU WILL NEED

A needle ✳ An egg ✳ A tiny moonstone
✳ Sealing wax or modeling clay

TIMING

The night of the crescent moon

THE SPELL

✳ With the needle make a small hole in the eggshell, draining out all the fluid.

✳ Make the hole just large enough to slip in the moonstone.

✳ Place the egg on an indoor window ledge.

✳ Unless medically forbidden, make love whenever you wish.

✳ On the full moon night, make love, and as you reach mutual orgasm, call out (silently if your partner is leery of spells), *Lady Moon, we ask of thee, keep our new child this night, safe within my partner/me.*

✳ Afterward, insert the needle into the eggshell hole, sealing the needle in place with sealing wax or modeling clay, and repeating the spell words.

✳ The next morning, bury your egg beneath a thriving plant.

A White Flower Waxing Moon Spell to Turn Friendship into Love

YOU WILL NEED

A glass or silver-colored bowl, half-filled with water ✳ Small white flowers or blossoms ✳ A smooth pointed stick or a crystal wand ✳ A silver ribbon

TIMING

When the moon is shining

THE SPELL

* Outdoors, move counterclockwise around the bowl seven times, encircling it with white flower petals, then dropping seven petals into the water.

* Stir the water seven times counterclockwise with the stick. As you do so, say, *Moon of increase, let love grow, that* [Name] *may increasing love show. Shine down on us your silver light, and make me beloved in his/her sight.*

* Leave the moon water overnight.

* In the morning, when you wake up, sprinkle seven drops of moon water over the ribbon, tie the ribbon in a bow, and wear it or carry it hidden for seven days, and thereafter when you know the person you like will be present.

A Crescent Moon Ritual for Reconciliation, When You Have Separated

YOU WILL NEED

Two silver candles ∗ A dish of rosemary,
which signifies love remembered

TIMING

The crescent moon and the three days afterward

THE SPELL

∗ Surround the candles with a counterclockwise circle of rosemary, saying,
*I create this circle of love and happy memories, to call back love and what
still can be, with the rising of the moon.*

∗ Light the candles from each other, repeating the spell words.

∗ Into each candle, sprinkle a few grains of rosemary, saying,
*Anger, bitterness, jealousy, burn, burn away. With the rising of the
moon, come back to me.*

∗ Blow out the candles and repeat the spell for three more nights,
adding a circle of rosemary moving outward each night.

∗ Leave the candles to burn down on night 4. Scatter the rosemary
from a window, saying, *With the rising of the moon, come back to me.*

A Waxing Moon Love Calling If You Are Attracted to a Neighbor Who Doesn't Seem to Notice You

YOU WILL NEED

Two moonstones

TIMING

Any night in the week before the full moon

THE SPELL

* When it is getting dark and you can see the moon, walk past your neighbor's house, pause, whisper his/her name, and softly say, *Winds from the sea, bring to me, love that will last, till time is past. Hear, love, hear, and give a sign, this moonstone I offer, hoping you will be mine.*

* Bury one moonstone outside or near the neighbor's property and carry the other moonstone with you.

* On a full moon night, bury the second moonstone near the first and find an excuse to ring the doorbell if your neighbor is at home, or phone him/her soon afterward.

A Waxing Moon Magnet and Mirror Spell to Attract an Unknown Lover

Seven silver candles * A round mirror, set flat on a
table * Pins * A horseshoe magnet * A pink fabric heart

TIMING

Before you go to bed

THE SPELL

* Set the lighted candles in a semicircle behind the mirror.

* Scatter the pins around the mirror, saying seven times,
  As pins are drawn like bees to flower, I call my love to me at this hour.

* Pick up all the pins with the magnet.

* Put the magnet and the attached pins on the fabric heart in the center
  of the mirror, saying, *Like moths to light, by day or night, send s/he
  who will be beloved in my sight.*

* Gaze down into the mirror in the candlelight, saying, *As moth to flame,
  my love I claim.*

* Blow out the candles.

* You may see your future love in the mirror afterglow.

A Three-Day Waxing Moon Ritual
If You Are Unlucky in Love

YOU WILL NEED

Three lemon or eucalyptus incense cones
* A silver heart locket on a thin green
thread * Strong green thread * A silver chain

TIMING

Anytime in the waxing moon cycle

THE SPELL

* On night 1, light one incense cone, passing the heart locket through the smoke three times, and say, *The link with bad love now I break. Good fortune and good love make.*

* Leave the incense to burn through.

* Remove the thin thread, leaving the heart locket in front of the incense cone.

* On night 2, light another incense cone, put the heart on the stronger thread, and repeat the spell words and actions.

* On night 3, light the last incense cone, put the heart on the silver chain, and repeat the spell, but add, *I shall find that loving heart, good fortune in love and a new start.*

* Leave the incense to burn through.

* Wear your heart on the silver chain when you go out or engage in online dating.

A Full Moon Fertility Ritual If You Are Trying to Conceive a Baby

YOU WILL NEED

A small bonfire or fireproof container outdoors, in which you can start a small fire ✳ Three small twigs, each larger than the first ✳ A silver-colored letter opener ✳ A moonstone

TIMING

As darkness falls

THE SPELL

* Into the fire, cast the smallest twig, saying, *Flame and fire, fertility inspire, that I/my partner may give birth to our child, before the fire is lit anew, when nine months are through.*

* Repeat the spell words and actions with the second-largest twig, and then the largest twig.

* Make love, if possible, near the fire, and let the fire burn through.

* Place the letter opener, touching the moonstone, in a sheltered place overnight.

* In the morning, scoop up the ashes and cast them into flowing water.

To Contact Your Twin Soul Telepathically at the Full Moon If S/He Has Gone Away and You Don't Know Where

YOU WILL NEED

A stick ＊ A basket ＊ Nine small fruits ＊ Nine white flowers
＊ Nine Chinese divinatory coins or small gold earrings

TIMING

*During the full moon, just before high tide,
by the ocean, a tidal pool, or a fast-flowing river*

THE SPELL

＊ Just below the high-tide line, with a stick draw a circle in the sand, enclosing your name and your twin soul's name, the hour, day, month, and year. Say, *I call my twin soul, by the power of the moon and the turning sea. Find me, wherever you may be.*

＊ Leave the basket, with the fruit, flowers, and coins, in the center of the circle, saying, *Twin Soul, I call across seas and land. My love, I reach out. Take my hand.*

＊ Hold your hands outstretched toward the sea.

＊ Leave the shore, and do not look back.

To Draw Down Full Moon Power for Restoring Passion to a Relationship

YOU WILL NEED

An isolated outdoor setting,
where the moon shines on water

TIMING

When the moon is bright

THE SPELL

* Face the moon, and raise your arms wide and high.

* Spin counterclockwise, faster and faster, saying, with increasing speed and intensity, *Draw down the moon, draw down the power. Lady Moon, your radiance shower. Draw down the moon, draw down the light, that my love and I may become one this night.*

* Continue until the moon seems to come rushing toward you and you get dizzy.

* If you partner is present, hold him/her tightly as you spin and make love under the moon, or seduce him/her where you are staying, with moon lust.

To Create a Moon Altar for Love

YOU WILL NEED

Four silver candles ✴ A table indoors or a large, round,
flat stone outdoors ✴ A bowl of water with sea salt
✴ A small silver knife ✴ Seven small moonstones
✴ Four jasmine or myrrh incense sticks

TIMING

*Make the altar at the full moon, but use it
during any moon phase*

THE SPELL

✴ Light a silver candle at each corner of the table or at four corners
of the large round stone.

✴ In the center, set a bowl of water in which you have mixed
three pinches of sea salt with a small silver knife.

✴ Put seven small moonstones in the water.

✴ Light a jasmine or myrrh incense stick in each corner.

✴ Trace the triple moon image, shown at right,
on the surface of the water with the knife.

✴ Face the moon, asking for help in love, and say,
May this be granted, by when next I see this moon
[or your own moon time line].

✴ Splash water on your brow, throat, and inner wrists, saying, *I would not
detain you, Moon, from your path. But first grant this love plea I ask.*

To More Formally Draw Down the Full Moon for Sex Magick

YOU WILL NEED

A moon altar (see previous spell) ✶ A silver letter opener or a small silver knife ✶ A bowl of salt water in the center of the altar

TIMING

During the full moon night

THE SPELL

* As one of you dips the letter opener in the water, raise the bowl to the moon, and say, *By seed and bud, by leaf and flower, I call your power, Lady Moon, to make my love and me as one.*

* Each in turn anoints the other with the salt water and blade, touching feet, knees, womb/genitals, and lips in silence.

* Rest the blade in the water.

* Spin around, holding each other tightly, faster and faster, making love until you become one with the moon.

* When you release your energies at the point of orgasm, call out your wish.

* Sit by candlelight and, before you leave, whisper *Mother Moon, grant this soon.*

A Waning Moon Ritual to Say Goodbye to a Love Going Nowhere

YOU WILL NEED

Jasmine tea or flowers, some soaked in salt water 24 hours before the spell, some unsalted ✳ A dark-colored beeswax or fast-burning pure wax candle, not dipped
✳ Moon flowers, mimosa, or jasmine

TIMING

During the later waning moon

THE SPELL

✳ Pour the salt water away after dark, retaining the herbs, and say,
Moon wane, moon drain from me, this love that grieves me bitterly.

✳ Light the candle, setting the salt-infused moon herbs in front of it.

✳ Drop a few unsalted jasmine petals or tea grains in the flame, saying,
Yet life can rise again, once I no longer love in vain.

✳ When the candle is melted, drop the salted herbs in the cooling pool of wax.

✳ Bury the pool of wax and plant moon flowers, mimosa, or jasmine on top of it.

A Waning Moon Banishing of a Destructive Lover Who Keeps Returning to Your Life

YOU WILL NEED

A dying white flower ✳ A pointed stick or
a piece of chalk and a chalkboard

TIMING

During the later waning moon, if possible on a rainy day

THE SPELL

✳ Around the flower, draw a square, either in earth or sand with a stick,
or in chalk on a chalkboard, saying, *These are the limits of your power,
these are the limits of your sway. You lose your thrall, away, now, away.
I no longer hear your call.*

✳ Leave the square to disappear if it's raining or erase the square, saying,
*See, I erase you from my life, your manipulation gone. Leave my life,
do not return. Your manipulation is done.*

✳ Cast the flower in any flowing water, unless it's destroyed by the rain.

A Waning Moon Oil Blessing If Your Partner Has Anger or Jealousy Issues

A silver candle * A lavender or chamomile plant
* A bottle of lavender, rosewood, or
vanilla essential oil * A diffuser

TIMING

Beginning the day after the full moon

THE SPELL

* Light the candle, touching your heart with your dominant hand, and say, *Grandmother Moon, as you grow less, grant to* [Name] *gentleness and peace. Take away anger, take away jealousy. Let these decrease.*

* Touch the plant with the same hand, repeating the spell words.

* Tap the lid of the bottle of oil with the same hand, saying the spell words again.

* Leave the bottle on an indoor window ledge.

* The next evening when you are alone, warm water in a diffuser, adding the oil, and say silently, *Grandmother Moon, let all anger and jealousy cease. Let there be in his/her mind and our lives peace.*

A Dark-Of-The-Moon Farewell If Your Love Has Died or Gone Away Forever

YOU WILL NEED

A purple candle ★ Dried vervain (use a split tea bag)
★ A bowl of warm water ★ A teaspoon of honey

TIMING

Beginning the night before the crescent moon

THE SPELL

* Light the candle and in the flame burn a few grains of vervain, saying,
  *I mourn your passing/leaving. My heart is grieving. Dark Moon,
  hold for me my sorrow deep within, that one day I can again begin.*

* Float the rest of the vervain in the water and stir it counterclockwise
  with the index finger of your dominant hand, repeating the spell words.

* Stir in the honey, saying, *Moon, when you appear once more in the sky,
  release my bittersweet good-bye.*

* Leave the candle to burn through and the next night, on the crescent
  moon, pour the honey water and vervain into a hole in the earth.

A Dark-Of-The-Moon Burial of a Bone of Contention If Neither of You Will Back Down

YOU WILL NEED

A trowel ✴ An animal bone or stone ✴ A permanent marker
pen or a sharp knife ✴ Rosemary or mint herb plants

TIMING

By the light of a small flashlight in darkness

THE SPELL

✴ With the trowel, dig a hole in the earth for your bone or stone.

✴ Write or scratch on your bone or stone a word or symbol to represent
the disagreement, saying, *It must be gone, it must be done. No easy
resolution or solution, and so this must be the final conclusion, and talk
of it no more.*

✴ Set the bone or stone in the ground, repeating the spell words.

✴ Cover the hole with earth, and in the soil on top, plant your herbs,
saying the spell words for a third time.

A Dark-of-the-Moon Unbinding
If Your Ex Intimidates You

YOU WILL NEED

A purple candle ⋆ A purple cord or
strong thread ⋆ A bowl of soil

TIMING

The first night of the dark of the moon

THE SPELL

* Light the candle.

* Tie a knot in the center of the cord, saying, *You,* [name your ex],
  *are bound from approaching me menacingly. Your intimidation shall
  now cease. By the power of fire, I order you, leave me in peace.*

* Hold the cord tightly at both ends with the center in the candle flame.
  Say, *Go from me, severed be. Now am I free. I cut the ties that bind.
  Your secret manipulation I unwind.*

* Drop the burning knot in the bowl of earth.

* Throw some soil over the candle to extinguish it.

* Throw the cord in the soil in the garbage.

To Bring a Secret Love out into the Open If You Are Tired of Keeping Your Love Hidden

YOU WILL NEED

Two silver candles ★ A silver letter opener
★ A fading white rose ★ A budding red rose in a vase

TIMING

The first day of the dark of the moon

THE SPELL

* Using the index finger of your dominant hand, trace invisibly on the side of the first candle your initials and those of your secret love. On the second candle, etch them with the letter opener so they are visible.

* Light the first candle, saying, *Enough of this secrecy, hiding in shadows, afraid others will see. This hidden love no longer shall be.*

* Extinguish the candle.

* On a crescent moon night, light the second candle, saying, *Now is the time for you to acknowledge me. If your love is true, this you must do.*

* Leave the candle to burn through. Throw away the white rose.

A Twenty-Eight- or Twenty-Nine-Night Moon Ritual to Resolve Problems That Keep You from Marrying

YOU WILL NEED

Twenty-nine silver tea lights ★ Twenty-eight or twenty-nine pearls ★ A glass jar with a lid ★ String

TIMING

Beginning on the crescent moon, and continuing to the next crescent

THE SPELL

* Light the first tea light and set a pearl in front of it, saying,
  Day by Moon Day, I ask this precious love shall grow, overcome the obstacles and resolution show.

* Put the pearl in the jar. With the lid on, shake it seven times, repeating the spell words seven times.

* Each night cast the spell, adding an extra tea light to form a circle, and replacing any lights that are burned through.

* On the final night, light all the candles, leaving them to burn through with the jar in the middle of the circle.

* String the pearls and give them as a necklace to your lover as a charm.

A Moon Cycle Ritual to Move Away with Your Love If You Need to Make Great Personal Sacrifices

YOU WILL NEED

Seven silver candles ✴ Seven jasmine or mimosa
incense sticks, one in front of each candle ✴ Seven silver
bells, suspended with silver thread from a plant

TIMING

Seven consecutive moon nights before you go

THE SPELL

* Light the first candle and the first incense stick, saying, *Much to regret, much to let go. As the Moon Days slip away, sorrow does flow.*

* Ring the first bell, saying, *But love calls, and loss can be gain. Though I must leave this old life, love will remain.*

* Leave the candle and incense to burn through and replace them with an unlit candle and incense stick in anticipation of doing the spell the next night.

* Repeat the spell for the next six nights, adding another candle each night, another incense stick, and ringing another bell.

* Take the plant and bells with you when you move.

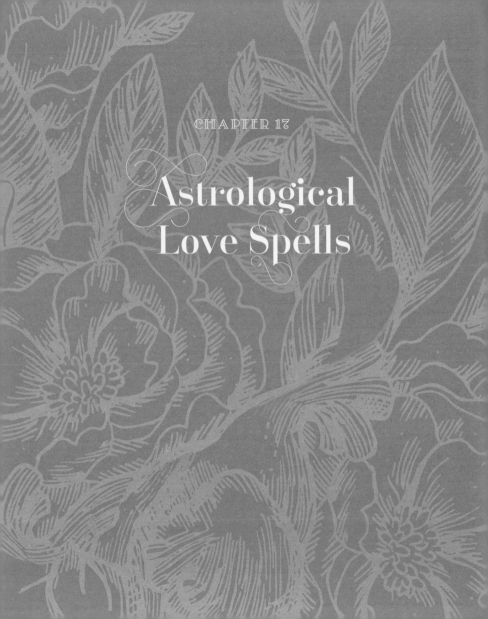

CHAPTER 17

Astrological
Love Spells

Many of us know our own zodiac sign and that of a partner. This forms a very powerful love energy, both during our own or our partner's zodiac sign period, when the full moon is in that sign (which happens once a year or every thirteen months) and when the moon is passing through one of the two relationship zodiac signs, for about two and a half days every month. This information is readily available online, in the weather or astrological section of any daily newspaper and in calendars and almanacs. Check the precise times for the astrological alignments for your own region.

Of course, regardless of yours and your partner's zodiac sign, you can use a particular zodiac period anytime to draw on its love energies when a specific power is needed. If you work when one sign is changing to another, you can benefit from the energies of both.

For the twelve zodiac signs, I have given the color, fragrance, crystal, and astrological glyph so you can apply these to any other rituals as well.

For astrological purposes, the sun and the moon are counted as planets, and powerful sun magick can be carried out at dawn, noon, and sunset.

A Dawn Sun Ritual to Heal a Bad Quarrel from the Night Before

Small, white stones, crystals, or clear glass
nuggets to make an astrological sun disk
on the ground large enough to stand on
* Sun disk

SUN GLYPH

TIMING

Beginning at or near sunrise

THE SPELL

325

* Stand in the center of your sun disk (see drawing
  at right), facing sunrise and raising your arms above
  your head with palms uppermost, and say, *This love
  like the day is reborn, last night's anger absorbed in the bright morn.*

* Swing both arms down behind your back, swing them forward,
  and clap your hands over your head, saying, *Sun as you climb higher,
  burn away last night's fire. Let us start over again, and your bright light
  take away bitterness and pain.*

* Leave the sun disk glyph in place until noon, and, in the meantime,
  make a gesture of reconciliation before noon, no matter who was
  at fault.

A Noon Ritual for Offering or Accepting a Lifetime Love Commitment

YOU WILL NEED

A gold-colored neck chain, ring, or gold earrings to give to your love ✳ A glass bowl of water, left in the sun from dawn to noon

TIMING

Between noon and 3 P.M.

SUN GLYPH

THE SPELL

* Face the sun and, holding the gold in your nondominant hand, draw the sun glyph nine times a few inches above it in the air with the index finger of your dominant hand, saying nine times, *As the sun reaches its height, I dedicate my love forever lasting. As long as the sun in the sky shines bright, this gold is my offering.*

* Sprinkle the water over and around the jewelry clockwise, repeating the spell words nine times.

* Give the jewelry to your partner when next you meet and pledge your lifelong commitment.

A Sunset Ritual for Accepting a Partner's Frailties and Giving up Trying to Change Him/Her

YOU WILL NEED

Four candles in a row, set in front of a mirror reflecting the sunset, (from left) orange, pink, purple, and yellow

TIMING

At sunset

THE SPELL

* On each candle, invisibly trace the sun glyph with your dominant hand.

* Light the candles left to right.

* Look through the candlelight at the mirror-reflected sunset, saying, *Though I know too well your weaknesses, yet I do not love you any less.*

* Extending your hands, held vertically, push your palms toward the mirror, and say, *Sunset, take away false hope and expectation. My love, I will stay with you forever, without hesitation.*

* Extinguish the candles in reverse order of lighting, afterward saying, *Reconciled am I to this choice, in your good qualities shall I rejoice.*

A Solar Eclipse Ritual for Putting behind You and Your Partner the Bad Times and Planning a Good Future Together

YOU WILL NEED

A place where you can see the full
or partial eclipse or watch it on
YouTube or another online source
* A smoky quartz or Apache tear crystal
* Two carnelian crystals

SOLAR ECLIPSE

TIMING

Just before the eclipse, until the sun fully reappears

THE SPELL

* As it gets darker, hold the smoky quartz crystal in your closed hands, saying, *The dark times, the sad hours, pass into darkness and lose their power.*

* In the darkness, add the carnelians to your closed hands, saying, *Bad memories eclipsed now shall be, returning light brings certainty.*

* As light returns, drop the smoky quartz crystal, slowly opening your hands to the returning light.

* Cast the smoky quartz crystal into water, leaving the carnelians in your garden or on a sunny window ledge to be filled with light.

A Lunar Eclipse Ritual for Letting Go of Feelings for a Former Lover That Keep You from Committing to a New Love

YOU WILL NEED

A purple candle ★ Seven myrrh incense cones ★ A bowl of soil ★ A silver candle

LUNAR ECLIPSE

TIMING

During a full or partial lunar eclipse

THE SPELL

* Light the purple candle as the moon disappears.

* Burn the incense cones embedded in the bowl of soil.

* When the moon has gone or partially disappeared, and the incense cones are ash, bury the ash deep in the bowl of soil, saying, *Old love die you must, as these ashes turn to dust. Eclipsed in darkness shall you be, old love, farewell, set me free.*

* When the moon starts to reappear, light the silver candle from the purple candle, and once full moonlight is restored, extinguish the purple candle, leaving the silver candle burning.

* Pour the bowl of soil into the earth.

A Blue Moon Ritual for Making a Seemingly Impossible Love Liaison Come True

YOU WILL NEED

Seven blue moonstones ⋆ A glass bowl of
water ⋆ The name of your desired love,
written over and over again in blue
ink on both sides of pale blue paper
⋆ Plants ⋆ A silver bag

TIMING

*Outdoors, during the second
full moon in a month*

THE SPELL

⋆ Drop the moonstones, one after the other, into the bowl of water,
saying, *Once in a blue moon cannot come too soon. This love I seek
some say cannot be, but the blue moon brings endless possibility.*

⋆ Fold the paper, putting it under the bowl, and say, *Rarely comes
this opportunity. Blue moon send my love to me.*

⋆ Leave the paper and water overnight in the moonlight and in
the morning pour the water onto plants.

⋆ Place the moonstones and the paper in the bag, saying,
Blue moon, bring this love to me soon.

When the Sun and the Moon Are Both in the Sky, for Helping Your Twin Soul Overcome Fear of Commitment

YOU WILL NEED

A black stone on which you have drawn in silver marking pen the moon glyph
∗ A white stone on which you have drawn in gold marking pen the sun glyph

SUN GLYPH

TIMING

*From crescent moon to full moon
(the spell is most powerful on the full moon)*

MOON GLYPH

THE SPELL

∗ Stand on a bridge over flowing water.

∗ Holding the moon stone in your left hand and the sun stone in your right, at the same moment release them into the water, saying,
*Sun and moon do share the sky. Our love is deep and will not die.
Trust even as the waters flow, that together forever happiness we'll know.*

∗ Buy a silver and a gold charm. Give the gold one to your future partner for courage.

An Aries Ritual to Encourage a Partner to Stand up to an Emotionally Blackmailing Ex-Partner

YOU WILL NEED

A red candle ✶ A cinnamon incense stick
✶ A red jasper crystal ✶ A lemon
✶ Whole cloves

ARIES GLYPH

TIMING

*Between March 21 and April 20, during
any Arian moon phase, or whenever you need
the courage of Aries*

THE SPELL

* Light the red candle and the incense, setting the crystal in front
  of the incense for the duration of the spell.

* Pierce the lemon skin all over with the cloves, saying, [Name], *No more
  your spite and false emotions, shall in our lives cause commotion. By the
  power of Aries, your blackmail shall cease. Feel the pain of what you do,
  and let this viciousness cease.*

* Hang the lemon outside the front door on a bush or tree until it decays.

* Hide the jasper under the doormat.

A Taurus Ritual for Domestic Harmony to Unite Stepchildren and Stepfamilies under One Roof

YOU WILL NEED

A few drops of rose essential oil, mixed with virgin olive oil ✳ A pink candle for each family member, including yourselves ✳ A planter with many budding pink roses

TAURUS GLYPH

TIMING

Between April 21 and May 21, during any Taurus moon period, or anytime you need the harmony of Taurus

THE SPELL

333

✳ Rub oil into each unlit candle, base to middle and top to bottom, but not around the wick, saying, *We shall harmonize as one family, though different we all may be. Tolerance and patience to one another show, so a united family shall grow.*

✳ Put the candles in a circle around the planter, drawing the Taurus glyph in the air over it.

✳ Light each candle clockwise, repeating the spell words. When they are burned through, set the planter in the center of your home.

A Gemini Twin Soul Ritual Where You Argue and yet Know You Are Right for Each Other

YOU WILL NEED

Two yellow candles ★ Two lavender incense sticks ★ A pointed citrine crystal ★ A bowl of lavender

GEMINI GLYPH

TIMING

Between May 22 and June 21, during a Gemini moon period, or whenever you need to call on the influence of Gemini

THE SPELL

* Light the candles and incense sticks.

* Spiral the incense, one in each hand, over each end of the crystal, saying, *We two are one, Gemini soul twins no doubt. So why do we bicker, niggle, and shout?*

* Blow out the candles, saying, *Strengthen the Gemini twin connection, so we both travel in the same direction.*

* Relight the candles, leaving the incense burning next to the crystal, and say, *Resolution shall there be, Gemini twin be patient with me, and I will more tolerant be.*

* Keep the crystal in a bowl of lavender.

A Cancerian Ritual for Restoring a Happy Home after a Jealous Friend or Relative Has Created Rifts between You

YOU WILL NEED

A silver candle ✳ A myrrh incense cone ✳ A dish of moonstones ✳ A clove of garlic on a small dish

CANCER GLYPH

TIMING

Between June 22 and July 22, during a Cancer moon period, or whenever you need to restore domestic tranquility

THE SPELL

✳ Light the candle and the incense in the center of the home, next to the dish of moonstones.

✳ Carry the dish of garlic from room to room, saying, *Take from here others' negativity, so we can live once more lovingly.*

✳ When you have visited every room, bury the clove of garlic near your property line.

✳ Carry the moonstones from room to room, then return them to the center of the home, saying, *Happiness is restored, bad feeling between us is no more.*

✳ Leave the candle and incense to burn through.

A Leo Ritual If Someone Is Trying to Steal Your Partner

YOU WILL NEED

A gold candle on which you etch with a letter opener the Leo glyph (see drawing) before lighting * An amber pendant or charm * A lighted diffuser, containing frankincense or orange essential oil

LEO GLYPH

TIMING

Between July 23 and August 23, during any Leo moon period, or whenever you need Leo to make sure you get noticed positively over all others

THE SPELL

* Light your Leo candle, passing the amber around it nine times clockwise, and say, *Mighty lion/lioness, make me shine that all will see, my love has eyes only for me.*

* Pass your amber through the fragrance, repeating the spell words.

* Hold the amber in your open, cupped hands, saying, *Leo power enter me now, I am the one to whom my love vows, lasting fidelity. Away any who would take him/her from me.*

* Wear or carry the amber charm when you meet your partner.

A Virgo Ritual for Disarming an Overly Critical Partner

YOU WILL NEED

A dark green candle on which the Virgo glyph
(see drawing) has been etched with a
letter opener ✳ A mint tea bag
✳ A mug ✳ A spoon ✳ A jade crystal

VIRGO GLYPH

TIMING

*Between August 24 and September 22, during any
Virgo moon period, or any time you need to call on
Virgo to withstand unfair criticism*

THE SPELL

✳ Light the candle, add boiling water to the tea bag in the mug, stirring
nine times counterclockwise.

✳ Leave the tea to steep for 10 minutes before straining the tea bag.

✳ Dip the crystal in the tea, saying, *You're always right, I'm always wrong.
I'm tired of your worn-out song.*

✳ Dip the crystal in the tea again, repeating the spell words nine times
in all.

✳ Wash the crystal in water, saying, *Your critical words, your carping tone,
your nit-picking stops or we are done.*

✳ Extinguish the candle and hide the crystal under his/her side of the bed.

A Libra Ritual If Your Partner Keeps Everyone Happy except You

Two blue candles ✶ Two blue lace agates ✶ A tub of vanilla ice cream, an ice cream scoop, and dishes

LIBRA GLYPH

TIMING

Between September 23 and October 23, during any Libran moon period, or whenever you need Libra to restore balance

THE SPELL

* Light one candle with the crystals in front of it.

* Fill dishes with ice cream, saying, *Hey, Mr./Ms. Ice-Cream Man/Gal, sharing with the world, and every dog, cat, and guinea pig, all your attention. How come I don't get a mention?*

* Light the second candle and scoop all the ice cream back into the tub, saying, *Hey, Mr./Ms. Ice-Cream Man/Gal, don't forget to see, I'd like some loving from you, just for me.*

* Leave the candles to burn through.

* Serve ice cream to you and your partner.

* Shake the crystals whenever your partner goes into Mr./Ms. Helpful mode.

A Scorpio Ritual If a Love Affair
Is Becoming Too Intense

YOU WILL NEED

An indigo candle with the Scorpio glyph
(see drawing) marked invisibly with
the index finger of your dominant hand
on one side ✳ A sandalwood incense stick
✳ An Andean or boulder opal, marked
invisibly on one side with the Scorpio
glyph ✳ A bowl of sand

SCORPIO GLYPH

TIMING

*Between October 24 and November 22, during any moon period in
Scorpio, or whenever you need Scorpio to remove intrusion in love.*

THE SPELL

✳ Light the candle and incense, and place the crystal in front of
the candle.

✳ Pass the incense around the candle and the crystal counterclockwise,
saying, *Your excessive attention totally freaks me, no longer so intensely
intrusive be.*

✳ Plunge the incense into the sand, lighted end down.

✳ Extinguish the candle, chop it up, crush the incense in the sand,
and dispose of them.

✳ Keep the opal between you and the overzealous lover.

A Sagittarius Ritual for Bringing Adventure into Your Lives at Any Age or Stage

YOU WILL NEED

Three orange candles in a triangle, set outside the paper ✶ Three sage incense sticks, one outside each candle ✶ A long strip of paper decorated with blue Sagittarian arrows pointing outward ✶ Three turquoise crystals set in a triangle in the center of the arrow paper ✶ Thread

SAGITTARIUS
GLYPH

TIMING

Between November 23 and December 21, during any Sagittarian moon period, or whenever you need the freedom of Sagittarius

THE SPELL

* Light the candles very fast and from each an incense stick, saying, *Arrows fly swift and swift return, for adventure and joy do we yearn.*

* Blow out the candles and the incense.

* Remove the crystals from the paper and hang the strip of arrows by an open window on a thread.

* Carry one of the turquoise crystals as a charm when you book your adventures.

A Capricorn Ritual for Caution If You Are Considering Throwing Away an Established Relationship for Sudden Passion

YOU WILL NEED

Three dice ✳ A lighted large brown candle
✳ Magnolia fragrance in a small dish
✳ A pointed green aventurine crystal,
set in front of the candle

CAPRICORN
GLYPH

TIMING

*Between December 22 and January 20, during any
Capricorn moon period, or when you need the wise caution of Capricorn*

THE SPELL

✳ Shake the dice, saying, *Dare I risk all? If I reach out to mad passion's call, will I fall?*

✳ Over the lighted candle and magnolia fragrance, draw invisibly with the aventurine point the Capricorn glyph (see drawing), saying *Wait, It's not too late, to preserve what for years we have worked hard for.*

✳ Put the dice away.

✳ Anoint your brow, throat, and heart with the magnolia fragrance, making the Capricorn glyph with the oil on your skin with the aventurine.

✳ Leave the candle to burn through.

An Aquarius Ritual for Detachment
If Your Partner Is Constantly Creating
Dramas over Trivial Matters

YOU WILL NEED

Five small, white, battery-powered
candles in a row ✱ A purple candle
✱ An amethyst soaking in water
✱ Dried rosemary in a dish

AQUARIUS GLYPH

TIMING

*Between January 21 and February 18, during any Aquarian
moon period, or whenever you need the detachment of Aquarius*

THE SPELL

✱ Turn on the battery-powered candles, saying, *Big dramas you create,
imagining catastrophes that just can't wait. Calm down, let it go.
Life's not a great big theater show.*

✱ Light the purple candle, setting the amethyst water in front of it and
sprinkling rosemary around it, and say, *Real life, needn't be a fight.
A tussle, panic, day and night.*

✱ Switch off the battery-powered candles, leaving the purple candle
to burn through, and say, *This is real. Let what will be, itself reveal.*

✱ Add amethyst-infused water to your partner's drinks.

A Pisces Ritual for Living Together Happily If You Have Different Priorities

YOU WILL NEED

A white wax candle, not dipped ∗ A red wax candle ∗ A heatproof tray ∗ Lemon juice ∗ Orange juice ∗ A jug ∗ Purple and green fluorite within the same crystal ∗ A letter opener or a knife

PISCES GLYPH

TIMING

Between February 19 and March 20, during any Pisces moon period, or when you need the Pisces integration of opposites

THE SPELL

∗ Light the candles close together on the tray so the wax mingles, saying, *Opposites together in compromise, in this difference happiness lies.*

∗ Mix lemon and orange juice in the jug, saying, *Not too sour, not too sweet, opposites together, blend and meet.*

∗ Hold the fluorite to the candlelight, saying, *Two colors within one stone, better together than alone.*

∗ From the mingled cooling wax, make a heart, etched with your entwined initials, and keep it with your crystal.

∗ Share the juice with your partner.

A Mercury Ritual for Starting Your Dream Venture with Your Partner, Based on Not Much More Than Hope

YOU WILL NEED

Five gold-colored coins
★ A yellow candle
★ A yellow citrine crystal
★ A dish of dried parsley

TIMING

Wednesday

THE SPELL

* Set the coins in an invoking pentagram formation (see drawing), tracing the shape invisibly with your dominant hand on the table and putting a coin on each visualized point.

* Set the candle and the citrine in the middle of the invisible pentagram and light the candle.

* Sprinkle a little parsley in the flame, saying, *Built on hope, built of dreams, and yet this will be a successful scheme. Swift Mercury, favor this speculation. Let us go forward without hesitation.*

* Leave the candle to burn through.

* Place the coins and the citrine, called the merchant's crystal, with any official papers, and, once you launch the venture, wherever you keep your petty cash.

A Mercury in Retrograde Ritual to Keep You or Your Partner from Making an Overly Hasty Decision

YOU WILL NEED

The Mercury in Retrograde sign
(see drawing), drawn in black on a small
square of white paper ✳ The Mercury
in Retrograde sign etched with a
letter opener or a sharp knife on a
half-burned and extinguished candle
✳ A small container, half-filled with water

TIMING

When Mercury goes into retrograde

THE SPELL

✳ Hold the paper, saying, *Now is not the time to act, nor decide. Let time reveal the course and facts, for now I* [or name partner] *put this issue to the side.*

✳ Push the paper into the water and freeze the container until Mercury moves forward again. Until then, refuse to be pressured.

✳ After the retrograde has ceased, relight your candle and let it burn through.

A Venus Morning Star Ritual for Moving On from a Broken Heart

YOU WILL NEED

A green candle ✳ A jade heart ✳ A copper
ring, necklace, or bracelet, Venus's metal
✳ Rose petals plucked from a fresh
pink rose ✳ A piece of soft silk

TIMING

*Friday morning, best if Venus
is in the morning sky*

VENUS GLYPH

THE SPELL

✳ Light the candle.

✳ Touch your heart first with the jade, then with the copper jewelry,
saying, *Only love can break a heart, only new love mend. Venus,
shimmering morning star, to me a new love send.*

✳ Put the crystal and copper in front of the candle, surrounding them
and the candle with rose petals, and say, *Only love can break a heart,
only new love can mend. Star of morning with your dawning,
let my heartbreak end.*

✳ Wear the copper jewelry.

✳ Wrap your jade heart in soft silk to ease your heartbreak.

✳ Let the candle burn through.

A Venus Evening Star for Dealing with a Partner Who Insists S/He Is Always Right

YOU WILL NEED

A citrus incense stick ✳ Six small copper disks or nails (from a hardware store) and six almonds, placed alternately in a circle ✳ A bowl of water

TIMING

Evening, preferably when Venus is in the sky

THE SPELL

✳ Light your incense, passing it around outside the circle of disks counterclockwise, and say, *Lady Venus, fierce evening star, my dogmatic partner does my happiness mar. No longer will I to this petty god/dess bow down, warrior Venus, his/her opinions drown.*

✳ Drop the copper disks in the water, leaving them as long as necessary until the copper turns green, then throw away the disks and the water.

✳ Feed the almonds to your partner or, if s/he is allergic, to the birds, saying/thinking, *By warrior Venus, I stake my claim. I express myself forcefully in your name.*

A Mars Ritual for Asking Someone Out Who You Fear May Say No

YOU WILL NEED

A red candle with the Mars glyph
(see drawing) etched on it with a letter
opener and a green candle with the Venus glyph
etched on it with the same tool ★ A red jasper
for Mars and a green jade for Venus ★ A dragon's
blood incense cone for Mars and a rose incense
cone for Venus, together in a dish
★ A drawstring bag

MARS
GLYPH

VENUS
GLYPH

TIMING

Tuesday, the day of Mars

THE SPELL

* Light both candles and incense cones.

* On the jasper, etch invisibly with your dominant hand the Venus glyph and on the jade the Mars glyph.

* Light both incense cones, pass both crystals together through the incense smoke, and say, [Name], *Let our energies be joined, it shall be so. If I ask you on a date, say yes not no.*

* When the incense cones are burned, put a little of the mixed, cooled ash and the crystals in a bag.

* Carry the bag when you ask the person for a date.

An All-Purpose Astrological Love Ritual
If Charts Say You Are Not Compatible

349

YOU WILL NEED

Two white candles ✻ A frankincense and a
myrrh incense stick ✻ A letter opener

TIMING

During a relevant zodiac period

THE SPELL

* On one candle, etch your astrological sign (see previous spells for the glyph for each sign) and your partner's astrological sign on the other, saying, *So love grows into compatibility, whatever the fortune-tellers say, our love will increase, and is here to stay.*

* Light each candle, in turn, holding each incense stick in each candle flame, in turn, and repeat the spell words.

* Holding the frankincense in your dominant hand and the myrrh in the other hand, draw in incense smoke first your astrological sign and then your partner's over the candles, saying, *Compatible we are and more compatible shall be, our starry love is for eternity.*

* Leave the candles and incense to burn through.

CHAPTER 18

Love Spells Calling on the Saints and Archangels for Help

Love spells calling on the angels and saints are especially powerful because they stem from a very old tradition. As we cast them, we can draw on the hopes and dreams of all who, through the centuries, have tapped into these energies.

For hundreds of years, people of many faiths, and none, have sought the help of the angels and saints to find and keep love. In the modern world, these folk spells have become updated but retain their essential power. As angel magick and saints and archangels card packs have become increasingly popular as oracles, so this form of love magick has been adopted increasingly by everyone from teenagers, in search of their first love, to those in their golden years who seek to revive a relationship or find a new partner in life. Saints' love spells are especially strong on particular days of the year associated with their festivals. Angel and archangel love spells are linked with specific days of the week or moon phases.

Indeed, many people have told me that when nothing else seems to work, appeals to these higher energies do produce good results.

A Seven-Archangel Spell to Honor a Significant Point in Your Relationship

YOU WILL NEED

Seven white candles in the formation shown below

TIMING

A significant date in your relationship, after dark

THE SPELL

* Light the central candle, calling Michael, archangel of the sun, saying, *I ask your blessings to bring lasting joy on this night, and so I call you Michael in this light.*

* Continue lighting the candles, changing the spell words for the different archangels.

* For candle 2, Gabriel, archangel of the moon, ask for *Twin Soul connections.*

* For candle 3, Camael, archangel of Mars, ask for *enduring strength.*

* For candle 4, Raphael, archangel of Mercury, ask for *fun and adventure.*

* For candle 5, Sachiel, archangel of Jupiter, ask for *lasting security and stability.*

* For candle, 6, Anael, archangel of Venus and roses, ask for *fidelity and gentleness.*

* For candle 7, Cassiel, archangel of Saturn, ask to *remain together in love all our days.*

* Leave all the candles burning.

An Adriel Angel Ritual for Helping You through Difficult Times in a Long-Term Relationship

YOU WILL NEED

Two pale blue candles * Two neroli
incense sticks * Any blue crystal

TIMING

The week after the full moon

THE SPELL

* Light the candles and incense sticks.

* Holding the blue crystal close to your lips, whisper the problems you are experiencing, and say, *Silvery misty Adriel, we are struggling. Within your wings enfold our sorrowing. I trust you to resolve everything.*

* Pass the incense stick smoke, one in each hand, over the crystal, now flat on the table, creating a veil of smoke around and over the crystal, and softly repeat the spell words.

* Carry the incense sticks outside, put them in earth, and leave them to burn away.

* Put your crystal in front of the candles, saying, *Adriel, bring light. Make all right.*

* Let the candles burn through.

* Bury the crystal where the incense ash is located.

An Atliel Angel Ritual for Increasing Passionate Love If Stolen Moments Are All You Have

YOU WILL NEED

Twenty-nine pieces of scarlet sewing silk
* Twenty-nine small silver bells * A tall indoor plant

TIMING

During a full moon night

THE SPELL

* Take lengths of silk, one by one, and tie a bell to each one.

* Knot each silk around the plant, saying, *Gold and silver Atliel, tonight your night of blazing fire, brings to me my love's desire. Make him/her not be able to resist. Let searing passion never desist.*

* When you have attached all twenty-nine bells and silks to the plant, one for each Moon Day, ring the bells one after the other, in turn, repeating the spell words faster and faster, until every bell on the plant is vibrating.

* Then cry out, *Atliel, angel, hear my call.*

* Make contact in any way possible.

A Second Atliel, Angel of the Full Moon, Ritual to Bring a Child into Your Life by Adoption or Surrogacy If You Are Meeting Obstacles

YOU WILL NEED

A small doll ✳ A large stamped, padded
envelope ✳ A silver pen

TIMING

During a full moon night

THE SPELL

✳ Hold the doll and say, *Atliel, our child/children wait to join my/our family, Yet I do not know where they may be. On this your night of fertility, in dazzling moonlight, make the pathway clear for me/us to see.*

✳ Put the doll in the envelope, seal it, and address it in silver ink to yourself/selves, saying, *Follow the angel, follow the moon, beloved children find your way home soon.*

✳ As soon as practical, mail the parcel.

✳ Make love under the moonlight.

An Anael, Archangel of Love, Ritual for Finding Lasting Love Later in Life

YOU WILL NEED

A tumblestone emerald, which is relatively inexpensive, or jade ✳ Six yellow roses in a vase

TIMING

Beginning Friday morning, for six days

THE SPELL

* Each morning, soak your emerald in a small cup of water, saying, *Anael, archangel of roses and lasting love, for me it is not too late, to find the twin soul who will make me whole. Yet I can no longer wait.*

* Each evening, add some emerald-infused water to the roses.

* Repeat the spell for five more days.

* On the seventh morning, put the emerald in the vase water, repeating the spell words.

* When the roses fade, scatter the petals, dry the emerald, and keep it beneath your pillow.

A Dirachiel Angel Ritual for Growing Love If a Friend Is Becoming More Than a Friend to You

358

YOU WILL NEED

A small silver medallion or moon charm
* White paper * A silver pen

TIMING

Around a crescent moon night

THE SPELL

* Hold the medallion/charm in your open, cupped hands under the crescent moon and facing any body of water.

* Say, *Dirachiel, with your crescent halo, this night I call you under your moon. Make* [Name] *see me as more than a friend. It is love I seek, that will never end.*

* Turn the medallion over three times in your hands, still facing the moon, and say, *Crescent moon, growing moon, moon in the stream, let me fulfill this my love dream.*

* Splash water on the medallion/charm.

* When the medallion/charm is dry, wrap it in the paper on which you have written Dirachiel's name in silver ink.

* On a full moon night, unwrap it and give the medallion/charm to your friend.

A Donquel Angel Ritual If You Are a Romantic and Won't Settle for Second Best

YOU WILL NEED

A heart- or circular-shaped silver-colored box ✳ Vanilla
potpourri ✳ Six hearts, cut from red paper or fabric,
each larger than the other ✳ A crystal angel

TIMING

Beginning Tuesday, for six days

THE SPELL

✳ Line the bottom of the box with potpourri, saying, *Donquel, with your scarlet sparkling wings, within this box I keep safe my heart, knowing you true love will bring. Angel of twin souls, send s/he who will make me whole, no other shall there be.*

✳ Put the largest heart in the box. Each day repeat the spell, adding the next-largest heart, so on day 6 all the hearts, in descending order of size, are inside the box.

✳ Add more potpourri and the crystal angel, repeating the spell words.

✳ Keep your Donquel box until love comes.

An Ergediel Angel Ritual of Lovers United to Hasten Matters If One of You Is Waiting for a Divorce

YOU WILL NEED

Sugar or honey * A dish of warm water
* A spoon * Small fruits

TIMING

The night before the full moon

THE SPELL

* Add the sugar/honey to the water, and stir with the spoon, saying,
  Ergediel, angel of shimmering gold, Our love is sweet to behold.
  Yet in secret must we meet. Hasten I ask resolution, so our love can
  have a happy conclusion.

* Add the fruits, saying, *Ergediel, unite us soon in love. Send your powers*
  from above. End delays, and open ways, so openly we can be together.

* Leave the water near an ants' or termites' nest, away from your home.

A Requiel Angel Grief Ritual for Loss after a Tragedy or Bereavement

YOU WILL NEED

Unpolished blue celestite, with holes in it, or blue selenite * A bowl of dying leaves or petals * Myrrh or lavender essential oil * A bowl of lavender potpourri

TIMING

During the end of the moon cycle

THE SPELL

* Gaze into the celestite, saying, *Once we were one, now I am left alone. Yet I cannot sorrow leave, my love, for you I daily grieve. Misty Requiel, ease the pain, bring me back to life again.*

* Put the celestite in the bowl of dying leaves or petals, and scatter most of the leaves or petals to the winds, repeating the spell words.

* Add a few drops of essential oil to the remaining leaves or petals, saying *the spell words for a third time and releasing the rest of the leaves or petals.*

* Take the celestite home, setting it in a bowl of lavender potpourri.

Index

About the Author

CASSANDRA EASON (Isle of Wight, England) is a best-selling author and a broadcaster on the paranormal. She has appeared many times on television and radio throughout the United States, Britain, Europe, and Australia. Cassandra originally trained as a teacher, and, while bringing up her five children, took a psychology honors degree with the intention of training as an educational psychologist.

A seemingly inexplicable psychic experience involving her two-year-old son Jack led to extensive research and the publication of a book on psychic children published by Random House in 1990. Since then, Cassandra has had more than 100 books published and translated into thirteen different languages. Cassandra also runs workshops in Australia and the United Kingdom and tours Australia each year. Many of her books have been serialized around the world and she has consulted with and contributed to such publications as the *UK Daily Mail*, *Daily Mirror*, *Daily Express*, *People*, *The Sun*, *News of the World* magazine, *Spirit and Destiny*, *Fate and Fortune*, *Prediction*, *Best and Bella*, *Homes and Gardens*, and *Good Housekeeping* and in *Woman's Day* and *New Idea* magazines in Australia. Cassandra now also regularly contributes to the UK magazine *Soul and Spirit*. She has long been acknowledged as a world expert on spellcraft and magick and has appeared many times on television and radio, including shows such as *Sky News*, ITV's *Strange but True*, BBC1's *Heaven and Earth*, and *Richard and Judy*, and she has also appeared in a series of mini films with Myleene Klass, and on Sky Living's *Jane Goldman Investigates*.